COMMERCIAL
MORTGAGES
101

COMMERCIAL MORTGAGES
101

Everything You Need to Know to Create a
Winning Loan Request Package

Michael Reinhard

AMACOM
American Management Association
New York • Atlanta • Brussels • Chicago • Mexico City • San Francisco
Shanghai • Tokyo • Toronto • Washington, D.C.

Bulk discounts available. For details visit:
www.amacombooks.org/go/specialsales
Or contact special sales:
Phone: 800-250-5308
Email: specialsls@amanet.org
View all the AMACOM titles at: www.amacombooks.org

Library of Congress Cataloging-in-Publication Data

Reinhard, Michael.
    Commercial mortgages 101 : everything you need to know to create a winning loan request
package / Michael Reinhard.
        p. cm.
    Includes bibliographical references and index.
    ISBN-13: 978-0-8144-1507-8
    ISBN-10: 0-8144-1507-5
    1. Mortgage loans—United States. 2. Commercial real estate—United States—Finance. 3.
Commercial loans—United States. I. Title.
    HG2040.5.U5R45 2010
    332.7'2—dc22
                                                                    2009031190

About AMA
American Management Association (www.amanet.org) is a world
leader in talent development, advancing the skills of individuals to
drive business success. Our mission is to support the goals of
individuals and organizations through a complete range of products
and services, including classroom and virtual seminars, webcasts,
webinars, podcasts, conferences, corporate and government solutions,
business books and research. AMA's approach to improving performance
combines experiential learning—learning through doing—with opportunities
for ongoing professional growth at every step of one's career journey.

Printing number

10 9 8 7 6 5 4

CONTENTS

ACKNOWLEDGMENTS

We all at one time or another dream of writing a book, but the reality is we often find ourselves too distracted with the demands of our family and careers. I'll be the first to admit that writing a book is no easy task. My motivation, courage, vision and faith in this project evolved over many years with the help of several dear friends, business associates, college professors, employers, coworkers and family. Each one of you has directly or indirectly contributed to the fulfillment of this dream.

First, I would like to thank Dr. Deborah J. Barrett, my technical writing professor at Texas A&M University, for giving me a big fat F on my mid-term grammar test. Not only did it humble me, it was a wake-up call that forever changed my attitude about writing. Thank you for not cutting me any slack. If it weren't for your hard-line and uncompromising dedication to the skill of technical writing, I might not have had the courage or confidence to write this book.

Next, I would like to thank Sally Caldwell, Associate Professor of the Department of Sociology at Texas State University, for her wise counsel, support, advice, and reassurance throughout the development of this book. Your consolation and mentoring gave me the fortitude to keep pressing forward.

Special thanks to real estate attorney Kim Lawrence of Dallas for his technical review and generous legal advice over the years. Thanks, too, to Kevin Marak and Mickey Jannol, two of the best and brightest in the business, for their technical review and editorial assistance.

I am immensely grateful to a dear friend of mine, Margarita Chavez, for her unwavering faith in my ability and for taking a special interest in my book. Thank you for reminding me every day not to give up.

Heartfelt thanks to my mom, Felicia McMahan, who loves and prays for me, and inspires me to never quit. And to my dad, Helmut Reinhard; my uncle, Conrad Kasselman; and my sister, Tina Thompson, for encouraging me to follow my heart, and reminding me that I always have family to lean on.

Last, but certainly not least, thanks to Bob Nirkind, William Helms, and Mike Sivilli of AMACOM Books, for believing in this project and helping me make this dream come true.

INTRODUCTION

Commercial Mortgages 101 is the culmination of fifteen years' experience in commercial real estate lending and credit analysis that began at the conclusion of the savings and loan crisis of the late 1980s and early 1990s. Toward the end of the savings and loan crisis that dominated the headlines for nearly a decade, commercial real estate lending was virtually nonexistent. Lending practices and underwriting policies once thought sound were now deemed completely unreliable. Eventually, a new breed of lenders rose from the ashes and reestablished the commercial real estate lending industry, transforming and setting in place new underwriting and credit standards still relevant today. *Commercial Mortgages 101* embodies this new establishment and attempts to provide a comprehensive overview of commercial real estate loans and fundamentals in underwriting and credit analysis. But before we discuss the contents within this book, a little history is in order.

The Tax Reform Act of 1986 and ensuing savings and loan crisis set in motion the beginning of the end for commercial real estate loans. Commercial real estate lenders were about to enter the Dark Ages, a decade-long systematic collapse and decline of the commercial real estate loan industry. From 1986 to 1995, the number of federally insured savings and loan institutions in the United States declined from 3,234 to 1,645.[1] This was primarily but not exclusively a result of unsound commercial real estate lending.[2] While they were not part of the savings and loan crisis, many other commercial banks failed during this time, as well. Between 1980 and 1994, more than 1,600 banks insured by the Federal Deposit Insurance Corporation (FDIC) were closed or received FDIC financial assistance.[3] The U.S. government ultimately appropriated $105 billion to resolve the crisis. After banks repaid the loans through various government interventions, there was a net loss to taxpayers of approximately $124 billion by the end of 1999.[4]

Although the savings and loan crisis of the 1980s and early 1990s seemed to have singlehandedly brought the commercial real estate lending industry to a halt, there were a few commercial banks and nonbank lenders such as life insurance companies and pension fund advisors that were still making commercial real estate loans, primarily refinances. But it wasn't until about 1993 that a new breed of commercial real estate lenders called conduit lenders emerged as a new source of commercial real estate loans, marking the beginning of a new era and forever changing the way commercial real estate loans are originated and underwritten. Conduit lenders, which were created by Wall Street investment banks, reignited the commercial real estate loan industry by providing a secondary market (called securitization) for mortgage banking firms, commercial banks, life insurance companies, and federal savings banks (successors of the savings and loan banks), a market that had never before existed. The commercial real estate lending industry, unlike years before, was now back in business.

With the advent of conduit lending or securitization came a new way of underwriting that was sorely absent during the era of the savings and loan turmoil. Stringent underwriting ratios and guidelines set by Wall Street investment banks during this time became the new standard for making commercial real estate loans among traditional banks or any other lender entering the mortgage banking business. Sound underwriting practices didn't just stop with the Wall Street banks; credit rating agencies such as Standard & Poor's, Fitch, and Moody's also provided further scrutiny before a loan was securitized. The adoption of this new underwriting standard by traditional banks and other nonconduit lenders has duly been cemented in the industry and now serves as the basis for understanding how commercial real estate loans are underwritten.

The commercial real estate loan industry is very complex and widely misunderstood by the average person. Even seasoned commercial real estate developers who borrow tens of millions of dollars fail to appreciate the difficulty in procuring a real estate loan. This fact is evident every time they are forced to solicit help from a commercial mortgage brokerage firm after months of unsuccessful attempts of their own. No matter who loans the money for the development, purchase, or refinance of a commercial property, whether it is a small-town building and loan institution like the one in the movie *It's a Wonderful Life* or a complicated consortium of private equity sponsored by a large Wall Street investment bank, the fundamentals of commercial real estate loans and underwriting remain the same. Therefore, the intent of this book is not to try to explain the intricacies and inner workings of today's complex real estate capital markets but to explain these fundamentals in a way that teaches the reader how to effectively think like a commercial real estate lender.

The book has three primary objectives. The first is to introduce the reader to the basics and fundamentals of commercial real estate loans. The second is to illustrate how both a borrower and a commercial real estate loan is underwritten and the third and most practical objective is to explain how to successfully prepare a comprehensive loan request package. This book is designed to appeal to a wide array of readers, including residential mortgage brokers, entry-level commercial mortgage brokers, novice real estate investors, college and university students, real estate instructors, and promoters and educators of real estate investment clubs and seminars, just to name a few.

The idea for this book came from years of dealing with novice real estate investors and residential mortgage broker clients in search of their very first commercial real estate loan. Typically, the average seasoned commercial real estate loan officer is solicited by professional commercial mortgage brokerage firms or institutional borrowers that employ teams of experts. Often these professionals prepare lengthy and comprehensive loan request packages (similar to a business plan) for the lender's review and approval. The purpose of the loan request package is to put everything at the lender's fingertips in a well-organized and persuasive prospectus for easy reference. Deviating from this method of loan solicitation only frustrates the lender and results in a game of phone tag between the lender and the broker in search of unanswered questions resulting from an incomplete package. Experience has shown that first-time commercial loan applicants, whether they are beginners or residential mortgage brokers seeking loans for themselves or for a client, often do deviate from this method. Many times they are inexperienced and unprepared to deal with the barrage of questions asked by the lender. Often a lender will simply reply to the broker's or investor's loan solicitation with a request of her own: "Well, just send me your loan request package, and I'll take a look at it."

In order to prepare a comprehensive loan request package, one must be knowledgeable in the field of commercial real estate loans.

Preparing and creating a loan request package is often left to the professionals, but if the borrower doesn't have a basic knowledge of commercial real estate loans and of the fundamentals of underwriting and credit analysis, he may find that creating a loan request package can be a daunting task. Though there are many books and schools that offer various courses in commercial real estate, there are none that combine an overview of commercial real estate finance, loans, and underwriting with real-world practical applications. Most real estate finance books are too technical or academic for the average real estate investor, leaving the reader intimidated rather than empowered. This book, however, is written in a conversational manner, as if someone were speaking to an audience for the first time with the specific goal of making them feel at ease or comfortable. The aim of the book is not only to educate the reader but to provide a step-by-step instruction manual for residential or entry-level mortgage brokers and real estate investors in search of their very first commercial real estate loan.

The book is divided into six chapters. Chapter 1 is primarily intended to provide the reader with an introduction to commercial real estate loans and underwriting. Chapter 1 is written with the beginner in mind, someone who is presumed to have no prior knowledge of or experience with commercial real estate or commercial real estate loans. The chapter begins by defining and explaining the word "mortgage" as it relates to the commercial real estate industry. (We also define the word "commercial.") This discussion is followed by a description and analysis of the different types of commercial properties. Midway through the chapter, the reader is introduced to the different types of commercial real estate lenders that originate and fund commercial real estate loans and mortgages. The reader is also introduced to common industry terms associated with a commercial mortgage such as "loan-to-value" and "amortization." The chapter concludes with an overview of the basics of commercial mortgage underwriting that are universal to all commercial real estate loans. Prior to reading Chapter 1, the reader is likely to have had some exposure to or experience with commercial real estate or commercial real estate loans during his career. For readers who have no experience with commercial real estate loans, Chapter 1 is a must-read, but for those with some level of experience, it should serve well as a refresher course. However, no matter what level of experience the reader may have had with commercial real estate loans, I highly recommend a review of Chapter 1 before moving on to Chapter 2.

After reading Chapter 1, the reader should be sufficiently well versed in the basics of commercial real estate loans and underwriting to start searching for his first commercial real estate loan. But before the search can begin, he must prepare a loan request package. By now you may be asking yourself what in the world is a loan request package and how is it prepared. Well, Chapter 2 answers that question and even walks you through the process step by step. For anyone who already has some experience in commercial real estate and who desires to break into the commercial mortgage brokerage business, Chapter 2 is the place to start.

We anticipate that many readers may be already in the process of searching for or attempting to broker a commercial real estate loan without a loan request package. Without a professional and well-prepared loan request package, you risk losing the lender's interest and may come across as extremely inexperienced, as well. The loan request package is very similar to a business plan and should always be used to make a good first impression with any lender.

Loan request packages are essential to any mortgage broker's or real estate investor's success. Length and quality of loan request packages vary, depending on the complexity of the real estate transaction. Unfortunately, they are often hastily prepared, rudimentary, and poorly written. No two loan request packages are alike, and not all of the information suggested or recommended in Chapter 2 is necessary in every case. Loan request packages can be as short as five pages or as long as forty pages. A professional and persuasive loan request package, one that is mostly likely to retain a lender's interest, has six sections: the executive summary, property description, location and demographics, economics, submarket data, and sponsorship. The sponsorship section of the loan request package as described in Chapter 2 is no more than a two- to three-page summary describing the borrower's net worth, liquidity, ownership experience, and real estate assets. Though words like "net worth" and "liquidity" may sound familiar, not everyone fully understands how they are calculated or used in underwriting. Because attributes such as these embody the essence of underwriting as a whole, we expand our discussion within a three-chapter section that begins with Chapter 3.

In general, the measure of financial strength and creditworthiness is based on a variety of factors that are not easily understood. It is often said that a person's net worth exists only on paper or that the person is house-poor or cash-poor. Adding to the confusion is the concept of liquidity. What does all this mean, and why does the lender need to know? All these issues and more are discussed in Chapter 3; the chapter looks at such topics as credit history, credit scores, personal cash flow, and banking and credit references. Even if a borrower passes the credit test, financial wherewithal alone is not enough to secure a loan. In addition to having a high net worth and an acceptable credit score, the borrower must have extensive experience in owning and operating commercial properties. The level of experience of any borrower is extremely important and cannot be overemphasized. Lenders in general are skeptical by nature and need quite a bit of convincing before they will make any kind of commitment to the borrower. So how can a lender be persuaded? Chapter 4 attempts to answer that question and also explores the way would-be borrowers can demonstrate ownership and management experience.

If, in fact, a borrower has extensive experience in owning and operating commercial real estate, it is reasonable to assume that a majority of the borrower's assets will be vested in real estate. Nothing persuades a lender more than an impressive portfolio of commercial income-producing properties. Generally speaking, net worth is derived primarily from the equity vested in a variety of assets, including cash, retirement accounts, personal property, business assets, and real estate; however, it's the real estate assets that are of most interest to the lender. The description and the market value of real estate assets listed on the assets side of the balance sheet are often just a sum total of a separate real estate schedule that provides greater details. This separate schedule or supplement to the balance sheet is referred to as the Schedule of Real Estate Owned or REO Schedule. What is a real estate schedule, and why is it so important? The answer to these questions and more, including a sample REO Schedule, can be found in Chapter 5, concluding our three-chapter series devoted to a borrower's financial strength, creditworthiness, and experience.

Another area of confusion and misconception in commercial real estate investing and lending relates to the different forms of ownership. Even though buying and investing in commercial real estate in one's personal name is less expensive and complicated than vesting title in a separate legal entity, both lawyers and accountants alike always advise against it. Purchasing and owning commercial real estate within legal entities such as limited liability companies and corporations is usually preferred over individual ownership. Whether for tax reasons or to minimize liability, certain forms of ownership are more likely than others to create complications for borrower and lender. Brokers and individual real estate investors often under-estimate the importance of legal ownership structures and the impact they have in shaping the loan. Chapter 6 addresses this issue head-on by first explaining the difference between a borrower and a borrowing entity and then offering an overview of nine different forms of ownership, presented in layman's terms.

The book overall is specifically written for the beginner whose knowledge of commercial real estate loans is limited. Underwriting commercial real estate loans is more art than science and is mastered only through years of back-office experience. The discipline of commercial real estate loan underwriting is further complicated by the fact that not every lender underwrites a loan exactly the same way. It would be unrealistic to assume that every type of property and every type of loan could be covered in just one book. Nevertheless, the fundamentals and the universal practice of commercial under-writing and credit analysis for any commercial real estate loan are common to just about every lender. The book is not intended to teach the reader how to be a financial analyst or a commercial underwriter overnight; it is more a user's manual to help those dealing with commercial real estate loans. Also, the book does not necessarily have to be read from cover to cover but can be referenced over time. Whether the book is read in its entirety or in part, the overall goal is to enhance the reader's skills in credit analysis, commercial underwriting, and loan solicitation. Whether you are a residential mortgage broker looking to break into the commercial mortgage brokerage business or a beginner real estate investor looking to transition from small residential properties to large commercial pro-perties, learning how to think and speak like a commercial real estate lender will put you on an even playing field with the professionals.

Notes

1. Federal Deposit Insurance Corporation Web site, http://www.fdic.gov/bank/analytical/banking/2000dec/ brv13n2_2.pdf.
2. Federal Deposit Insurance Corporation Web site, http://www.fdic.gov/bank/historical/history/vol2/panel3.pdf.
3. Federal Deposit Insurance Corporation Web site, http://www.fdic.gov/bank/historical/history/3_85.pdf.
4. FDIC Banking Review, "The Cost of the Savings and Loan Crisis: Truth and Consequences," Federal Deposit Insurance Corporation, December 2000, http://fdic.gov/bank/analytical/banking/2000dec.

COMMERCIAL
MORTGAGES
101

AN INTRODUCTION TO COMMERCIAL REAL ESTATE LOANS

Commercial properties are everywhere, in our neighborhoods, in our cities, and on every corner. There are probably just as many commercial buildings in the United States as there are single-family homes, and most likely just as many commercial real estate loans, too. Like residential properties, commercial buildings are built or purchased with borrowed money. Money borrowed for the construction, purchase, or refinance of a commercial property is commonly referred to as a commercial real estate loan or commercial mortgage. Commercial mortgages have nothing in common with single-family residential mortgages. They are like night and day. Even the professionals who engage in the origination and underwriting of commercial mortgages are distinct in every way from those who work in the residential mortgage industry.

Whether you are a novice real estate investor looking for your very first commercial real estate loan or a residential mortgage broker looking to venture into the commercial mortgage brokerage business, you will need to forget everything you know about residential mortgages. Terminology like "stated-income," "full-doc," "HELOC," "good-faith estimate," and "discount points," which are unique to residential mortgages, cannot be found in the lexicon of commercial mortgages. The commercial real estate loan industry is very complex and takes years to master. But mastering the industry doesn't have to take years, especially for those who wish to get a head start. Learning how and where to find a commercial real estate loan is what this whole book is about. Chapter 1 is an overview of commercial mortgages and the commercial real estate loan industry and begins by defining the terms "commercial" and "mortgage" in the context of commercial mortgages. Within this chapter you will find a discussion of the different types of commercial properties and commercial real estate lenders, including an explanation of typical financing terms found in every commercial mortgage. At the conclusion of this chapter you will be introduced to the methods and terminology used in underwriting a commercial real estate loan.

What Is a Commercial Mortgage?

The simplest definition of a *commercial mortgage* is basically this: a loan for the purchase or refinance of a commercial property. A commercial mortgage is similar to a residential mortgage, except the collateral is a commercial building, not residential.[1] However, to fully appreciate the complexity and broad use of the phrase, it is best to first separate the two words and define them independently.

"Mortgage" Defined

Most people think that a mortgage is the same as a loan and often use these words interchangeably without realizing the difference. The terms *mortgage* and *loan* have the same meaning in a colloquial sense, but, technically speaking, the two are not the same thing. A mortgage is actually a written legal document, referred to as a *mortgage instrument*, signed by a borrower who pledges his or her title to the property as security for the *loan*.[2] In other words, a mortgage is a written pledge by the borrower to the lender relinquishing the borrower's interest in the title to the property in the event of a default of the loan. The term "loan," on the other hand, refers to nothing more than borrowed money. The legal term for a mortgage lender is *mortgagee*, while the legal term for a borrower is *mortgagor*.

There are generally two types of mortgage instruments: *mortgages* and *deeds of trust*.[3] Both instruments create a *lien* against the title to the property and represent only a transfer of the borrower's ownership interest in the property either to a trustee or to a lender; neither is a transfer of the title itself. A *lien* is a legal claim of one person upon the property of another person to secure the payment of a debt or the satisfaction of an obligation.[4] In layman's terms, it is the right to take another's property if a debt is not paid in full. Not all states use *mortgages*. For example, both California and Texas use a *deed of trust* to create liens, while other states, including North Carolina and Georgia, use *mortgages*. Bear in mind we are talking about the type of *mortgage instrument* here. For example, just because Texas and California use a deed of trust doesn't mean that the lender is not creating a mortgage, as previously defined; it's just that different states have different names for the "mortgage instrument" itself.

States that use either a mortgage or a deed of trust are called "Lien Theory" states, meaning that both mortgage instruments create a lien against the title to the property rather than transferring title to the lender. Though both mortgage instruments create liens in the same way, it is the foreclosure process that sets them apart. A deed of trust differs from a mortgage in that in many states the property can be foreclosed on by a nonjudicial sale held by the trustee.[5] A non-judicial sale means that the trustee on behalf of the lender can go straight to the courthouse steps and conduct a foreclosure sale of the property without permission from any court. The foreclosure process can be much faster for a deed of trust than for a mortgage. Foreclosure processes that involve a mortgage almost always require court approval before a lender can proceed with the sale of the property to satisfy the debt.[6] It is also much more time consuming and costly to foreclose on a property using mortgages.

States that allow the lender to actually possess or hold title to the property until the loan is paid in full under the old English common law system are called "Title Theory" states. The best example to explain the concept of Title Theory is a car loan. When a person buys a car, the lender actually holds the original title until the loan is paid in full and then returns the original paper title to the owner stamped "paid in full." There are only six states that still use the old English common law type of mortgage: Connecticut, Maine, New Hampshire, North Carolina, Rhode Island, and Vermont. In "Lien Theory" states, title to the property is actually held by the borrower for the benefit of the trustee and the lender until there is a default under the loan. In the event of a default, the trustee then forecloses on the lien on behalf of the lender.

Mortgages are created only for real estate, which is why mortgages and deeds of trust are recorded in the real property records of county courthouses. You will never hear a car loan, a business loan, a personal loan, or any kind of non–real estate debt referred to as a mortgage. Mortgages today are exclusively used for both residential and commercial real estate loans, which may explain why the home loan industry and residential brokerage firms prefer to use the word "mortgage" rather than the word "loan." Despite what may have become natural for you to say, teach yourself to start thinking like a professional and begin associating the word "mortgage" with the words "lien" and "deed of trust." In summary, if you really like using the term "commercial mortgage" because it is natural or easy to say, always remember that what you are really describing is a *commercial real estate loan.*

"Commercial" Defined

If you look up the word "commercial" in the dictionary, you will find that there are many definitions, depending on the context of the usage. But what is crystal clear is that the word has no association with real estate in any way. "Commercial" is derived from the root word "commerce," which has more to do with trade and business than with real estate. So what does the word "commercial" really mean when it is associated with mortgage or real estate? In the context of this book, the word "commercial" can be best defined as meaning "not residential." *Residential properties,* as defined by Fannie Mae, are limited to single-family homes and multifamily dwellings of four units or fewer, such as duplexes, triplexes, and fourplexes. It is because of this very narrow definition that we find the word "commercial" convenient, because if the property is not a single-family home, a duplex, a triplex, or even a fourplex, what other alternative do we have but to classify it as commercial?

So up to this point we can safely say what a commercial property is not. What then is a commercial property? As long as it doesn't meet the Fannie Mae definition of a residential property, a commercial property can be any type of building or parcel of land used for any commercial purpose. In other words, if it is not a single-family home, a duplex, a triplex, or a fourplex, then it is simply a commercial property. Why is this significant? It's important because commercial properties and commercial mortgages are as vast as the oceans that separate the continents, and this is where residential mortgage brokers and novice real estate investors underestimate the complexity of the industry. Unlike the residential mortgage industry, which is largely regulated by Fannie Mae, the commercial mortgage industry is fragmented and extremely inconsistent. Commercial properties and commercial mortgages can be simple or extremely complex, depending on the property type.

Not all commercial properties are alike. There are a variety of income-producing and non-income-producing properties that qualify for loans and some that do not. Whether or not a particular commercial property type qualifies for a loan also depends largely on the type of lender. This is why it's best to first become familiar with the many types of commercial properties and their subsets. Lenders can be very fickle, and you will learn quickly that not all commercial lenders like the same kind of commercial properties. Some lenders will lend only for apartments, while others will lend only for office buildings, so it's critical that you understand how to identify a commercial property and properly describe it to the lender. If you don't know what kind of commercial property it is or what it is used for, you will soon lose your credibility with the lender and possibly the lender's interest altogether.

Typically, a commercial building is the lender's only collateral or security for the repayment of a commercial real estate loan. The type, condition, age, size, and quality of the commercial building must be described in detail for the lender's consideration. You may think that's easy to do. After all, there's no difference between a retail center and a shopping center; they're all the same anyway, right? No, they're not. For example, there are many variations of shopping centers, such as grocery-anchored centers, non-grocery-anchored centers (also referred to as strip retail centers), shadowed anchored centers, neighborhood shopping centers, com-

munity shopping centers, big-box power centers, shopping malls, and single-tenant and high-end specialty or boutique centers. Lenders actually apply different interest rates and financing terms according to the type of retail center. For example, interest rates are usually lower for a grocery-anchored shopping center than they are for a small strip retail center. This is why broad knowledge of the different types of retail centers is important; it can mean the difference between a high interest rate and a low one. There are hundreds of types of commercial properties too numerous to mention, but what we can do is highlight those commercial property types that are most commonly sought after by commercial real estate lenders.

Types of Commercial Properties

Commercial real estate lenders make loans on real estate for one and only one compelling reason: because there is cash flow from the property to pay back the loan. However, not all *commercial properties* generate cash flow. For example, an unused or unoccupied vacant tract of land does not generate cash flow though it is still called a commercial property. Because cash flow is essential with any loan, the collateral (land and buildings) must first be identified as either a property that generates cash flow or one that does not. *Commercial properties* that generate cash flow are referred to as *income producing*, and properties that do not are referred to as *non-income producing, or owner-occupied.* Understanding this distinction between income-producing and non-income-producing properties is key in establishing the foundation on which the commercial real estate lending industry is built.

Non-Income-Producing Properties

The term "non-income-producing" specifically refers to the absence of a lease. In other words, the property is not rented or leased to a person or business, and the commonly assumed relationship between landlord and tenant does not exist. A tract of land with or without a commercial building on it whose owner is not receiving rent or any other consideration is simply referred to as a "non-income-producing property." Another term for "non-income-producing" is "owner-occupied," which means that the company or business occupying the land or commercial building happens to be the owner of the land and building as well as the owner of the business. In this situation, the business owner is relying on the income from the business to pay his or her commercial mortgage payments to the lender and not to a landlord. A business owner who occupies his or her property for the sole purpose of owning and operating a business is simply referred to as an *owner-occupant*.

Owner-occupied buildings are free-standing single-occupant buildings that are occupied by the property owner. These buildings are usually designed and built specifically for the type of business the owner is running. For example, a muffler shop is built with equipment intended specifically to lift automobiles up off the ground so that a mechanic can fix and replace mufflers; an automatic car-wash facility is specifically designed and built to wash cars. Both buildings are commercial properties, but they are owner occupied and do not have any cash flow from rents because there are no tenants. The only cash flow associated with the property is from the operation of the business itself, such as income from customers' payments for parts and labor for the muffler repair or the income from washing cars. Owner-occupied properties have neither a landlord nor tenant. There are small business owners that are owner-occupants, and there are large companies that are owner-occupants, such as Wal-Mart and Target. These large retail companies do not pay rent because they typically own their own buildings. Examples of other non-income-producing properties that may or may not be owner-occupied include the following:

Churches	Day care centers	Gas stations	Schools
Car dealerships	Marinas	Auto repair shops	Factories
Amusement parks	Hospitals	Nursing homes	Car washes
Zoos	Convenience stores	Airports	Museums
Truck stops	Cemeteries/funeral homes	Auto race tracks	Golf courses
Bowling alleys	Business condos	Casinos	Time shares

Income-Producing Properties

The term "income-producing" specifically refers to the presence of a lease. In other words, there is a landlord-and-tenant relationship in which the owner of the property (the landlord) leases the property to a tenant. The phrase "income-producing," from the perspective of a lender, suggests that the cash flow used to pay back the loan will be derived from monthly rent paid by the tenant to the landlord. The landlord, in turn, takes the money that he or she receives from the tenant and uses it to pay back the loan.

It is important to emphasize that the owner of the property (the landlord) owns the property for no reason other than to make money by leasing the property to business owners who are interested in only renting and not owning. Notice the mutually exclusive benefit between landlord and tenant. Landlords don't want to own and operate a business, and business owners (tenants) don't want to own and take care of a building. The landlord's expertise is in owning and operating commercial real estate, not the businesses that occupy their buildings. Likewise, tenants can focus on running their business without the worry of maintaining and operating a building.

Commercial real estate lenders, like landlords, are experts in understanding the commercial real estate market and thus are willing to loan money to a landlord. What commercial real estate lenders don't understand and prefer not to loan money for are the very businesses that occupy the buildings. Why? The reason is that business cash flow is a hundred times more difficult to understand. The practice of lending to businesses is an entirely different industry and often left to bankers who specialize in commercial and industrial loans. Commercial real estate, on the other hand, in the eyes of the commercial real estate lender, is a commodity that is easier to analyze and much more predictable.

Commercial properties that are designed and built specifically to be occupied by businesses that are unrelated to the landlord are referred to as "investment properties." Landlords buy income-producing properties as an investment because of the anticipated positive cash flows and capital appreciation. These positive cash flows are supposed to represent both a return *of* capital and a return *on* capital to the landlord. It is for this somewhat predictable cash flow that lenders desire to loan money to landlords. Commercial real estate lenders that try to loan money to owner-occupied commercial properties must be able to understand the business and what it is that the business does to generate revenue to ensure that the loan can be repaid, which is very difficult. Unlike the income-producing property, the owner-occupied property has as its only source of cash flow the profit of the business, not the rent. If the lender can't understand the business, then it is less likely to loan money for the building. There are lenders that lend to these types of commercial properties, but not nearly as many as the number of lenders that desire to lend on income-producing properties.

Single-Tenant Properties

Income-producing commercial properties can be either single-tenant or multitenant properties. In the lexicon of commercial real estate, the term "single-tenant" always refers to a landlord-and-tenant relationship, even though it may appear that the building is owner-occupied.

Single-tenant properties are solitary free-standing structures, built on single parcels of land. Most single-tenant properties have long-term leases because of the specialized use and design of the property. These properties are usually leased prior to their construction and are rarely built based on speculation. A developer will agree to develop the site or construct the building in exchange for a long-term lease with the tenant. You probably have seen those signs posted on vacant tracts of land that read "Build to Suit." What that means is that the owner of the land, usually a developer, desires to build a structure specifically for an end-user who agrees to lease the property from the developer for a specified amount of time, say ten to twenty years. The developer will spend his or her own money to construct the building and then will lease it to the user. Rarely will a developer build a single-occupant building without having first entered into a contract with a specific user who agrees to rent the property after construction. This is the only scenario in which a lender will give the developer the construction loan. Unless a developer has more than enough cash sitting in the lender's vault to cover the loan, a typical lender will rarely loan money for the construction of a speculative building. Examples of income-producing single-tenant properties include the following:

Toys 'R' Us	Bed Bath & Beyond	Hobby Lobby	Big Lots
Walgreens	Kohl's	Dollar General	Garden Ridge
Best Buy	CVS Pharmacy	Academy	Firestone Tire
Costco	Blockbuster Video	Staples	Office Depot

Multitenant Properties

Multitenant properties usually are occupied by two or more tenants with shorter term leases, lasting two, three, or five years. Multitenant properties are considered to be much more flexible than single-tenant buildings because they are designed to provide a variety of store spaces and sizes in proximity to large anchor tenants. Large anchor tenants like Krogers serve as a major draw for other smaller tenants. Tenants have specific space and visibility requirements, and if the building doesn't have what the tenant is looking for, the tenant will go elsewhere.

The advantage that a multitenant building has over a single-tenant building is that there is less risk associated with the disruption of cash flow in the event of an unexpected vacancy. Having two or three tenant vacancies in a multitenant building is not all that unusual. The same does not hold true for single-tenant properties. Whenever a single-tenant property loses a tenant, the property becomes 100 percent vacant, resulting in zero cash flow.

Another advantage of a multitenant property is that its economic life span is much longer than that of single-tenant property. Multitenant buildings are adaptable to ever-changing retail trends, unlike single-tenant buildings, which are designed specifically to meet a tenant's need at that time. Circuit City and Mervyns are examples of single-tenant buildings designed for a specific retail use that were closed and are now sitting empty.

Both single-tenant and multitenant properties have their inherent risks, but lenders usually deal with those potential risks in their underwriting and make adjustments to compensate themselves for the risks. For example, lenders usually limit the amortization period of a single-tenant property to a maximum of twenty years if the tenant's primary lease term is only five or ten years. The reason for a shorter amortization is that the lender wants the loan paid down as quickly as possible because there's no guarantee that the tenant will be in business ten or fifteen years down the road. Finding a replacement tenant for a single-tenant or special-use building takes a long time and therefore presents a greater risk to the lender. However, this is not the case for multitenant buildings. Loans for multitenant buildings often have amortization periods up to thirty years because of their versatility and longer economic life.

There are many types of multitenant properties, but they are usually differentiated among their own classification. Commercial properties are generally divided into six classifications, with further sub-classifications. This is the standard used by commercial real estate lenders when quoting and pricing a loan. With regard to classification, single-tenant buildings are actually treated as a subclassification within each of the six general classifications. The six general classifications of commercial properties, along with their subclassifications, are as follows:

1. Retail
   - Grocery-anchored shopping center
   - Strip center (unanchored)
   - Community center
   - Neighborhood center
   - Big-box power center
   - Regional mall
   - Single-tenant

2. Office
   - High-rise (downtown)
   - Midrise (suburban)
   - Medical office building
   - Single-tenant

3. Multifamily (apartment)
   - High-rise
   - Midrise
   - Garden-style

  ➤ Condominium

  ➤ Mobile home park

4. Industrial-warehouse
   - ➤ Office warehouse
   - ➤ Office-flex
   - ➤ Self-storage/mini-warehouse
   - ➤ Light manufacturing
   - ➤ Distribution facility

5. Hospitality (hotel and motel)
   - ➤ Full-service
   - ➤ Limited-service
   - ➤ Extended-stay
   - ➤ Resort

6. Special purpose
   - ➤ Senior/independent living
   - ➤ Assisted living
   - ➤ Skilled nursing facility
   - ➤ R&D (research and development)

Types of Commercial Real Estate Lenders

Commercial real estate loans are originated by thousands of different types of lenders, either through correspondent relationships or directly to the borrower. "Loan origination" is an industry term that refers to the underwriting and funding of a loan. When a lender says that its company originated $2 billion in loans, it is the same as saying that the lender underwrote and funded $2 billion in loans. Commercial real estate lenders primarily originate new loans using two distinct methods. The first and most common way is through correspondent relationships. The second method is by dealing directly with the borrower.

Correspondent relationships can be exclusive or nonexclusive. A correspondent relationship is nothing more than an exclusive right given by the commercial real estate lender to an independent, third-party company, such as a mortgage banker or mortgage broker, for the purpose of marketing and originating new loan business for the lender. The best example of a correspondent relationship (and historically the only way that commercial real estate loans were originated for many years) involves life insurance companies. Beginning in the 1950s, these companies saw an opportunity to reinvest hundreds of millions of dollars in cash generated from their insurance premiums into commercial real estate loans. However, they needed help in finding high-quality commercial real estate developers and borrowers that were actively building and investing in the same quality of commercial properties. From that need emerged the commercial mortgage banker. The job of a commercial mortgage banker was to search for qualified developers and borrowers who were looking for financing on behalf of the life insurance company. These commercial mortgage bankers and brokers acted as the liaison between the life insurance companies and the borrowers in sort of a matchmaking role. Using the life insurance company's money, a commercial mortgage banker merely table funded the loan in exchange for a fee for originating and underwriting the loan. Those relationships were usually exclusive, meaning that the only way a borrower could contact the life insurance company was through the mortgage banker who had the exclusive right to represent that company. Correspondent relationships still exist, but they are now few and far between.

Today, with the advent of the computer and the Internet, commercial real estate lenders are less dependent on correspondent agencies to source and find new loans. Commercial real estate lenders today are multifaceted finance companies with a network of regional and branch offices from which to market their loan products. Even some of the large life insurance companies that once were closed off to the general public are now dealing directly with anyone that needs a commercial real estate loan. Exclusive correspondent relationships are now on the decline, and, unlike in decades past, both borrowers and mortgage brokers have unrestricted access to a vast array of commercial real estate lenders.

Generally speaking, commercial real estate lenders are separated into seven classifications: banks, life insurance companies, conduit lenders, agency lenders, credit/finance companies, mortgage bankers, and private lenders.

Banks

Commercial banks are the usual lenders of choice for most borrowers. That may not be surprising, since you can't drive your car without running into a bank branch on any given street corner. There are basically three types of banks, which really are not that distinctively different when it comes to originating commercial real estate loans. The first type is a *commercial bank*. Deposits of a commercial bank are insured by the Federal Deposit Insurance Corporation (FDIC). These banks are either state chartered, meaning they can do business only in their home state, or federally chartered, meaning they can conduct business across state lines (federally chartered banks are also known as national associations).

The second is a *savings bank*, or *federal savings bank*, which is a remnant of the former thrifts (called savings and loans or sometimes thrift and loan), whose deposits were insured by the FSLIC (Federal Savings and Loan Insurance Corporation). The federal government took over the thrift industry when the Federal Savings and Loan Insurance Corporation went bankrupt in the early 1990s after the savings and loan crisis. As a result of the savings and loan bailout, the government required all remaining savings and loan institutions to be renamed "savings bank." Today, the deposits of a savings bank are insured by the Deposit Insurance Fund (DIF).

The third type of bank is a *credit union*. A credit union is a cooperative financial institution that is owned and controlled by its members. Any person who has an account is a member and part owner of a credit union. Credit unions are distinctively different from commercial banks and other financial institutions because they are not open to the general public and are often not-for-profit cooperatives. Deposits of a credit union are insured by the National Credit Union Share Insurance Fund.

No matter which type of bank you are dealing with, the one thing all three have in common is that they all rely upon customer deposits to fund their commercial real estate loans, which explains why depository institutions such as banks and credit unions are heavily regulated by the federal government. There are other sources of capital that banks use to fund commercial real estate loans. These include borrowing from other banks or from the Federal Home Loan Bank. Imprudent or risky real estate lending can lead to a bank's insolvency or, worse, bankruptcy. Banks usually offer shorter loan terms, shorter amortizations, and higher floating interest rates than other types of lenders. In addition, they invariably require a *full guarantee* by the borrower, meaning that the borrower agrees to unconditionally guarantee full repayment of the loan. The advantage that banks have over other lenders is that they can be flexible with their loan terms, including eliminating prepayment penalties or monthly escrows for real estate taxes, insurance, or repair reserves.

Life Insurance Companies

Life insurance companies are the second biggest source of commercial real estate loans. In the past, life insurance companies offered lower interest rates than most other types of lenders because of their low leverage. Today, however, the opposite holds true. Life insurance companies are now charging rates 2 to 3 percentage points higher than usual rates, thanks to the subprime mortgage crisis and the ensuing global financial crisis that plagued the world's economy starting in 2009. Credit and loans for commercial real estate nearly dried up during this period, and most life insurance companies raised their prices to compensate them for the risk.

Life insurance companies make loans using the money they collect from the premiums they receive for the life insurance policies, fixed-income annuities, and other financial products they sell. Unlike banks, life insurance companies are not regulated by state or federal banking oversight agencies and can make loans without any restrictions. However, despite this lack of oversight, they are extremely conservative underwriters and lend only on high-quality commercial real estate properties, usually limiting loans up to a maximum of 75 percent of the appraised value.

Life insurance companies are extremely risk averse, and thus they tend to look for brand-new or well-located properties in major metropolitan cities. There are small life insurance companies that lend as little as $500,000 and large life insurance companies that lend up to $100 million per transaction. Life insurance companies can be very creative and offer many types of loans for many different types of properties, which is why mortgage bankers and brokers rely heavily on life insurance companies. As mentioned earlier, there are many small and medium-size life insurance companies whose names you may not know that use exclusive correspondents for sourcing and originating loans. Larger life insurance companies that are still actively making commercial real estate loans, names that you may recognize, include Allstate, New York Life, MetLife, and John Hancock.

Conduit Lenders NO!.

A *conduit lender* is typically a New York Wall Street investment bank like Morgan Stanley, JPMorgan Chase, or Goldman Sachs, which through a distinct and separate division of the bank originates, underwrites, and funds commercial real estate loans the same way that residential mortgage bankers or commercial banks do for residential loans. Investment banks fund conduit loans using their own money or borrowed money from large commercial banks, like Bank of America, Citigroup, and Wells Fargo. Conduit loans are individual commercial mortgages that are pooled and transferred to a trust for securitization (the process of taking a pool of commercial mortgages and converting them into fixed-income securities called commercial mortgage-backed securities or CMBS). This is almost identical to the way that residential loans are pooled by Fannie Mae and then converted to mortgage-backed securities (MBS). These securities, also referred to as bonds, are separated into different bond classes according to a grading system that factors in yield, duration, and payment priority. Credit rating agencies like Fitch, Standard & Poor's, and Moody's then assign credit ratings to the various bond classes, ranging from investment grade (AAA through BBB–) to below investment grade (BB). Once bonds are classified and given a credit rating, they are packaged and sold to institutional investors such as banks, foreign governments, and life insurance companies.

Wall Street investment banks primarily make their money from underwriting, creating, and selling fixed-income securities, which are then sold by bond dealers on the open market. These securities or bonds are secured and backed by the commercial mortgages, and the commercial mortgages are secured by the property such as an office building or retail center. The best way to explain how a conduit loan works is by working backwards. A conduit lender begins by using its own cash or borrowed money, for example, from a line of credit from a big commercial bank like Citibank. The conduit lender, which can be a Wall Street investment bank or an unrelated independent mortgage bank, then loans the money to a borrower who needs it to purchase an office building. The term of the loan is ten years, meaning that there is a balloon payment at the end of ten years. The investment bank or mortgage bank is now the owner of that promissory note (the note). However, the investment bank cannot keep the note for ten years because it borrowed the money from Citibank using a loan with a very short term of two years. The conundrum for the investment bank or mortgage bank is that it will take ten years to get its money back from the borrower, but in the meantime Citibank wants its loan paid off within two years. To solve that problem, the investment bank then creates a fixed-income security or bond that is secured by the commercial mortgage. The fixed-income security is then sold to a long-term investor who doesn't mind holding a ten-year bond. The money from the sale of the bond is then used to pay back the loan from Citibank. The investment bank makes its money when the bond is sold. Let's say that the value of the original commercial mortgage was $5 million, which was the face amount of the loan given to the borrower. The investment bank in turn sells that same mortgage, packaged as a long-term bond, for a higher price of $5.1 million, thus making a profit of $100,000. The higher price represents a 2 percent premium paid by the long-term institutional investor. Selling bonds at a 2 percent premium, along with other underwriting and securitization fees, is how conduit lenders make their money.

You may be wondering why a long-term investor would pay more for the bond than the face amount of the mortgage. To be able to answer that question, one needs to understand the nature of bond markets. Simply put, bond investors are after yields, regardless of price. Higher demands for securities mean higher prices. Paying a higher price lowers the yield to the bond investor, but that is how the bond market works. This process is what provides liquidity to the mortgage industry and competition among commercial real estate lenders. Higher competition among conduit lenders translates into lower interest rates. The advantage of conduit lenders is that their loans are typically *nonrecourse.* Nonrecourse loans do not require personal guarantees, thus releasing the borrower from personal liability. In addition, they offer very low long-term fixed interest rates, longer amortization, and higher loan-to-value ratios. The disadvantage is that these loans are extremely rigid and expensive to originate. It is also very difficult to pay off a conduit loan early, and even when the loan can be prepaid early there are huge prepayment penalties. In fact, most of these conduit loans have lock-out periods for years before the loan can be prepaid in part or in whole.

Agency Lenders multifamily only properties

Agency lenders are privately owned or publicly traded commercial mortgage banking firms that originate, underwrite, and fund commercial real estate loans with their own money or with money borrowed for the sole purpose of selling these loans back to one of the two government-sponsored agencies: Federal National Mortgage Association (Fannie Mae) and Federal Home Loan Mortgage Corporation (Freddie Mac). Agency lenders, however, lend money only for residential-related commercial properties such as multifamily homes, senior housing, assisted living, student housing, and manufactured housing. Fannie Mae and Freddie Mac were specifically created by the federal government to provide a secondary market for both single-family and multifamily loans, which in turn provides greater liquidity and affordability within the housing market.

Unlike investment banks (conduit lenders) that make their money selling bonds backed or secured by these commercial mortgages, agency lenders (commercial mortgage banks) make their money originating and underwriting commercial real estate loans by charging a loan origination fee of 1 percent. They then sell the loans to Fannie Mae or Freddie Mac *para pasu*, meaning that Fannie Mae or Freddie Mac purchases the loan at the coupon rate or face value of the note. If the loan amount is $1 million, then Fannie Mae pays $1 million.

An agency lender primarily makes its money by charging processing, underwriting, and loan origination fees. Agency lenders also make money servicing the loans they sell to Fannie Mac and Freddie Mac. Loans originated by agency lenders are underwritten using strict Fannie Mae or Freddie Mac underwriting guidelines. Agency lenders that fail to follow these strict underwriting guidelines risk having their loans rejected. When a loan is rejected, the commercial mortgage bank is essentially stuck with the loan. It can either sell the whole loan to another bank or private lender or just hold on to it. Agency lenders must have years of underwriting and servicing experience and be extremely well capitalized to participate in originating and selling commercial loans to Fannie Mae and Freddie Mac.

Because of the stringent financial and capital requirements, Fannie Mae and Freddie Mac have limited the number of preapproved agency lenders to about twenty-seven nationwide. These twenty-seven are approved by Fannie Mae as Delegated Underwriting and Servicing lenders, or DUS lenders, which is a special designation with many privileges. Loans purchased by Fannie Mae and Freddie Mac are pooled, packaged, and converted into commercial mortgage-backed securities (CMBS) the same way conduit loans are converted to bonds. In fact, the very securitization process that conduit lenders use today was originally created by Fannie Mae for the residential mortgage market. The commercial mortgage industry began emulating Fannie Mae's securitization process in the early 1990s.

Credit Companies

Credit or *finance companies* are wholly owned subsidiaries or financing divisions of large corporate investment-grade companies. General Electric (GE) is a perfect example of a global international company that owns such a company. GE Capital is a division of GE that makes commercial real estate loans, equipment loans, and business loans, just to name few.

Credit and finance companies are extremely well capitalized, meaning that they have very large balance sheets and that they, unlike banks, can lend their own money without oversight or restrictions imposed by the government. Credit companies, however, often borrow money for their financing activities. The cost of borrowing money is very cheap because of the parent company's extremely high credit and debt rating. For example, GE's corporate credit rating is AAA, which allows it to borrow at very low interest rates. GE's subsidiary, GE Capital, also has access to this cheap money. This money is then reinvested by way of commercial real estate loans at higher interest rates to the general public.

Ratings agencies like Standard & Poors, Moody's, and Duff & Phelps assign debt ratings to credit companies on the basis of their liquidity and financial strength. A company that is considered highly desirable by institutional investors has a minimum debt rating of BBB or higher. The highest possible rating is AAA+. Companies with the highest debt ratings can issue corporate bonds, or commercial paper, at a very low pay rate. This ability to borrow money or raise capital at extremely low interest rates is what gives them an advantage over banks. Loans originated by credit and finance companies are either held as portfolio loans or securitized like conduit loans.

Mortgage Bankers

Mortgage bankers are in business to originate and fund commercial real estate loans for the sole purpose of collecting an origination fee. A mortgage banking firm typically funds the loan with its own money or with money borrowed through a large line of credit with a commercial bank and then sells the loan. Mortgage bankers typically sell these loans to Wall Street investment banks and government agencies such Fannie Mae and Freddie Mac.

Some of these bankers actually fund the loan with their own money via a credit facility at a commercial bank or with private funds. Mortgage bankers that do not have access to commercial credit lines or that lack the funds often table fund. *Table funding* is an industry practice that allows a mortgage bank to originate, process, underwrite, close, and record real estate loans in their own name on behalf of an unrelated third-party lender. The closing package and loan documents are simultaneously assigned to the unrelated third-party lender when funds from the third-party lender are wired to the title company. The mortgage bank often, but not always, services the mortgage on behalf of the third-party lender, as well. Table funding is a way to keep a mortgage bank's borrowing costs to a minimum. However, mortgage banking firms usually must take a portion of the risk loss if they want to table fund. A mortgage bank that table funds is actually not the lender. What the mortgage bank is really doing is only originating, underwriting, and servicing these loans. The actual lender remains anonymous. Mortgage bankers make their money by charging loan origination and loan servicing fees. Loan servicing is the business of collecting the monthly mortgage payment and escrows from the borrower on behalf of the note holder. Other loan-servicing duties include enforcing loan covenants and paying real estate taxes and property insurance premiums on behalf of the borrower.

Private Lenders

Private lenders are companies that raise money or capital by soliciting individual investors through a process called *syndication*. Syndication is a method used by private lenders to create a debt fund that can be used to make commercial real estate loans. Private lenders are very opportunistic and usually promise high returns to their investors in exchange for their money. The anticipated high returns usually require interest rates higher than those available from other kinds of lenders. Private lenders are often referred to as hard-money lenders because of their high interest rates. Private lenders are often lenders of last resort. Borrowers are from time to time forced to seek alternative financing when properties do not qualify for traditional financing offered by banks or conduit lenders. There are many reasons why loans are declined by traditional lenders, but that doesn't mean that the property is not eligible for some kind of loan. There are many types of private lenders, some hard-money and some not. Private lenders are not regulated by any state or federal agency, nor are their deposits insured. In general, private lenders usually are willing to take a greater amount of risk when lending their money. They can be creative and often lend at higher loan-to-value ratios than other sources or lend on properties that have high vacancy rates and little or no cash flow.

Commercial Mortgage Terms

There are six basic components or financing terms common to all commercial mortgages: the maturity date, the amortization period, interest rate or note rate, loan-to-value, pre-payment penalty, and recourse provision. Collectively, these six components are simply referred to as "loan terms." Financing terms or loan terms are usually first introduced or quoted when the lender issues a letter of intent. A letter of intent is a written preliminary loan proposal providing a summary of each of the six financing terms and conditions that will be made part of the promissory note. Alternate names and variations among loan terms often make it difficult to size a loan, so it's important that the meaning and relevancy of each financing term is fully understood before quoting and underwriting a commercial real estate loan.

Maturity Period

A commercial real estate loan must be paid off in full at some point in time, in other words the loan eventually matures and ceases to exist. The phrase "maturity period" refers specifically to the life span of a loan. Loans never live on in perpetuity. The *maturity period* of a commercial real estate loan is very similar to that of a residential loan, with only a few exceptions. A loan can mature slowly over time, or it can end abruptly. A loan that has a very long life span and that matures slowly over time to the point that the loan balance is reduced to zero is referred to as a *fully amortizing* or *self-amortizing loan*. The maturity period of a fully amortizing loan always equals the length of the amortization period. A loan that has a short life span and matures abruptly is referred to as a *term loan*. The life span or maturity period of a typical term loan ranges from one to fifteen years. Term loans are not self-amortizing and require a large lump sum payment at the end of the maturity period, referred to as a *balloon payment*. Unlike a fully amortizing loan, the maturity period of a term loan never equals the length of the amortization period.

The maturity period of a commercial real estate loan is typically much shorter than a residential mortgage. However, nearly all residential mortgages are basically self-amortizing, so there's not much more that can be said about the differences. Nevertheless, a short maturity period always requires a balloon payment. A balloon payment is an indication that the loan is not fully amortizing. The amount of the balloon payment is usually equal to the amount of the outstanding balance. It is also important to point out that the calculation of monthly principal and interest is the same for both a fully amortizing loan and a term loan. The only difference between the two is the maturity date. For example, the monthly payment of a term loan with a maturity period of ten years and an amortization period of thirty years is no different than the monthly payment of a thirty-year fully amortizing loan. This type of loan is referred to as a *10/30*. The monthly payment of principal and interest for the ten-year loan is calculated on the basis of 360 months, just like a thirty-year fully amortizing loan. The only difference is that the ten-year loan will eventually have to be refinanced. The maturity periods of a typical term loan are three, five, seven, or ten years. Apartment loans are the only exception; you can find fifteen, twenty, or thirty-year fully amortizing terms, but rarely will you find a fully amortizing term for a nonresidential commercial property such as an office building or retail center.

Amortization Period

The word "amortization" refers to the process of gradually reducing a debt over time through a series of periodic payments, usually in increments of calendar months. The length of time it takes to fully amortize a loan is referred to as the *amortization period* and is often set or predetermined by the lender. The calculation of monthly payments of principal and interest is also dependent on this period of amortization. The period of amortization should not be confused with the maturity period of a loan. The maturity period of a loan is actually dependent on the length of the amortization period, not the other way around. The maturity period of a loan will never exceed the amortization period.

Periods of amortization for commercial real estate loans can range from ten years up to forty years, and in the case of construction loans or bridge loans there often isn't any amortization at all. A loan without amortization is referred to as an *interest-only loan*. The monthly payment of an interest-only loan is pure interest, with no principal reduction. Most lenders refrain from the use of interest-only loans because of regulatory requirements. Bank examiners do not like interest-only loans, especially if the cash flow is more than sufficient to support an amortizing payment. Interest-only loans are typically reserved for ground-up construction loans and for interim financings on commercial properties that are in need of significant repairs or have insufficient cash flow. The average period of amortization is thirty years, or 360 months. The interest portion of a monthly payment principal and interest compounds monthly, which is why amortization is stated in months instead of years.

Loan-to-Value Ratios

Loan-to-value ratios, or *LTVs*, for commercial real estate loans are typically 80 percent or less. Loan-to-value is the relationship, expressed in a percentage ratio, between the loan amount and the property's market value. For example, if a property has a market value of $1 million and the loan is $800,000, then the loan-to-value ratio is 80 percent ($800,000 ÷ $1,000,000 = 0.80 or 80%). Commercial real estate lenders are much more conservative than residential lenders and are less willing to risk lending money above 80 percent of a property's value. There are many other lenders who are willing to lend above the 80 percent standard threshold, but this willingness comes with a price. Lenders who push leverage limits often require a higher percentage of equity participation in exchange for accepting the extra risk. Equity participation simply means that the lender will receive a specified preferred return on the extra leverage including a share of the appreciation in the equity. You may think these are hard-money lenders, but that is not typically the case, because hard-money lenders usually lend at lower LTVs.

The word "value" in the term "loan-to-value" usually means the "as-is" appraised value. It is also important to note that a lender must use the lower of "as-is" appraised value or actual cost, if the loan is for the acquisition or purchase of a property. It is important to make a distinction between cost and value. *Cost* is the actual purchase price plus any capital improvements, whereas *value* is only an appraisal of value. Lenders recognize this distinction and will always draw attention to the apparent difference between the two values in their underwriting. Specifically, for a purchase loan, the standard 80 percent LTV is actually 80 percent of the lower of either actual cost or the appraised value of the property. If the loan is for a refinance and the borrower has owned the property for at least a year, then cost is not considered and the appraised value can be used. In general, the practice of lending on the basis of or using the appraised value when the actual cost or purchase price is lower than the appraised value is a regulatory violation that commercial banks would rather do without.

Interest Rates

Commercial interest rates quoted by commercial real estate lenders are determined by applying or adding a margin to a standard index. The margin is commonly referred to as a spread. A spread represents the gross profit or gross margin over and above the lender's cost of funds. Spreads also represents the gross margin over and above an alternative investment with an identical maturity period, such as a five-year or ten-year U.S. Treasury bond. Spreads are expressed in terms of basis points such as 175 or 200; 100 basis points equal a single percentage point. For example, a spread of 150 basis points is the same as 1.5 percent. An index can be a published market rate of interest or yield on a particular government bond such as a ten-year U.S. Treasury note, or it can be an average of overnight lending rates among the world's largest banks. The index and the spread together make up the whole interest rate. There are only three types of indexes used by lenders: U.S. Treasury yields, the *Wall Street Journal* prime rate, and the London Interbank Offered Rate, referred to as LIBOR.

The maturity period of a loan usually dictates how interest rates are calculated. If the maturity period of a loan is ten years, the interest rate will be based on the corresponding yield of a ten-year U.S. Treasury bond, referred to as the ten-year Treasury index. On top of this index, the lender will add its overhead and operating costs, loan-servicing fee, and profit margin to create the actual interest rate of the loan. For instance, if the yield of a U.S. Government ten-year Treasury note is 3.5 percent, the lender will add an additional interest rate of 2 percent plus a loan-servicing fee of 0.85 percent to arrive at an overall interest rate for the loan of 6.35 percent. This example is simplified, since lenders actually use basis points to calculate retail interest rates. This is just one illustration of how commercial interest rates are quoted.

Another market index commonly used by lenders instead of a U.S. Treasury yield is the U.S. *prime rate*. The U.S. prime rate is the base rate on corporate loans posted by at least 70 percent of the ten largest U.S. banks as published in the *Wall Street Journal*.[7] A bank's prime rate is the most competitive or the lowest interest rate offered to its most valuable corporate clients and high-net-worth customers. Nevertheless, commercial real estate lenders still frequently pad this rate by adding a premium of 1 or 2 percent in order to establish a retail interest rate for the loan. Depending on how competitive the market has become for the best clients, banks may offer loans at the prime rate without any premium. Other banks use the LIBOR as the index, plus a spread of 2.0 percent to 4.0 percent. LIBOR is the British Bankers' Association average of interbank offered rates for dollar deposits in the London market as published in the *Wall Street Journal*.[8] It is an overseas index that U.S. banks like to use. A fourth market index used by lenders, not yet mentioned, is an *interest rate swap spread*. Similar to the other indexes, a commercial real estate lender will add an additional 1 percent to 3 percent to an interest rate swap spread. Interest rate swap spreads are derived from complicated derivative contracts. These derivative contracts, which typically exchange or swap fixed-rate interest payments for floating-rate interest payments, are an essential tool for investors, who use them to hedge, speculate, and manage risk.

Prepayment Penalty

Commercial real estate lenders make loans because they need to invest their money in exchange for an anticipated rate of return. This rate of return is essentially the interest rate that they charge on the loan. If a lender makes a loan that matures in ten years, the lender assumes that it will receive without any interruptions monthly payments of principal and interest for the entire ten years. It's because of this expectation of the lender that *prepayment penalties* were created. Prepayment penalties are essentially deterrents to the early or premature payoff of the loan prior to the maturity date agreed to by the lender and the borrower.

There are three types of prepayment penalties that are commonly used by nearly all types of commercial real estate lenders. The first is *yield maintenance,* which is a very complex algebraic calculation used by Fannie Mae, conduit lenders, and life insurance companies. In a nutshell, it means that the earlier you try to pay off the loan, the higher the penalty. For example, the prepayment penalty on a typical ten-year loan term that is prepaid within the first five years of the ten-year loan term can range from a steep 6 percent to 10 percent of the loan amount. Of course, as the loan nears the maturity date, the prepayment penalty diminishes.

The second kind of prepayment penalty is *defeasance*, which is mostly used by conduit lenders. Defeasance is actually not a prepayment penalty but a very costly way to pay off the mortgage early. Defeasing a loan is a very complicated process of substituting one form of collateral for another so that the bondholders do not lose their income stream. The bondholders are ultimately the last ones who end up possessing the mortgage from the original lender via a commercial mortgage-backed security (CMBS). What is actually happening when a loan is defeased is that the mortgage is paid off but instead of the cash proceeds going straight back to the bondholder, the money is actually spent on the purchase of a series of U.S. fixed-rate securities (fixed-rate bonds) that provide a stream of monthly cash flow identical to the stream of principal and interest payments used to pay the bondholder prior to the release of the mortgage. The idea behind defeasance is to make it very difficult for the borrower to pay off the loan early because bondholders are long-term investors. Defeasance is just as expensive as yield maintenance, involves the use of lawyers, and can take several months to implement.

The third and least complicated prepayment method is a *fixed* or *step-down (declining) schedule*. This method is the simplest to understand and the least expensive. The prepayment penalty is fixed at a constant percentage rate for each year during the life of the loan. For example, a loan with a maturity period that ends within five years may have a prepayment penalty of 2 percent for each year, but this is rare. What is more common, in contrast to a fixed schedule, is a step-down schedule (also called declining prepay). The penalty of a step-down schedule may start at 5 percent during the first year of the loan term and then step down to 4 percent during the second year, to 3 percent during the third year, and so forth until the fifth year of the loan. All three prepayment methods usually allow the borrower to prepay the loan without penalty during the last three or six months of the loan term. This is referred to as the *open period*.

Recourse vs. Nonrecourse Loans

The issue of recourse versus nonrecourse loans is always a concern for borrowers seeking commercial real estate loans. A sophisticated borrower, especially one who has many partners, usually desires a nonrecourse loan. The term "nonrecourse" means that the borrower is not personally liable for any lender's losses associated with a fore-closure of the property. Essentially, a nonrecourse loan is a mutual agreement between a borrower and a lender that in the event the bor-rower defaults on the loan for any reason, the lender's only legal recourse is for the sale of the property via foreclosure, even if there is a loss. However, the borrower is not entirely off the hook if the lender's losses are the direct result of nonmonetary defaults such as fraud and misrepresentation. A recourse loan is the opposite; the borrower is unconditionally responsible for the full repayment of the loan and any deficiency or loss incurred by the lender.

Commercial Mortgage Underwriting

Underwriting a commercial real estate loan is a two-step process. Think of commercial mortgage underwriting as a two-prong fork. The first prong deals with the borrower, or what some lenders like to refer to as the *sponsorship*, and the second prong deals specifically with the property's cash flow, commonly referred to as *property under-writing*. In other words, a commercial real estate lender must underwrite the borrower as well as underwrite the property. The discipline of underwriting the borrower is completely different than underwriting the property. Sponsorship is just another way of referring to or describing the borrower. The origin of the word is not known, but a guess might suggest that years ago it was a description of the actual individual or person who acted as the ringmaster or promoter who raised money for an investment opportunity. Property underwriting focuses specifically on the property's financial performance and requires a thorough review of both historical and current cash flow. Though the topic of sponsorship (underwriting the borrower) is briefly mentioned in the discussion that follows, it is property underwriting that is our main focus for the remainder of this chapter.

Sponsorship

Underwriting commercial real estate loans, unlike underwriting residential mortgages, is not driven by FICO scores.[9] In other words, a borrower's FICO score is not central or key to the approval of a commercial real estate loan, as it is for residential loans. While a borrower's FICO score is important to a certain extent, in the eyes of a commercial real estate lender it is often considered less reliable than other factors in assessing the overall credit risk. A low FICO score itself is not necessarily a reason for declining a commercial real estate loan, since there are many factors behind the scoring system that a commercial real estate lender considers innocuous. For example, in the eyes of a commercial real estate lender, late payments and collections can ruin a borrower's creditworthiness more than would an unusually high number of inquiries or high credit balances. However, extenuating circumstances and detailed explanations are often taken into consideration by lenders, thus negating the face value of a low credit score that otherwise would have had a direct negative impact on loan approval. Nevertheless, a high score usually makes the credit decision easier for the underwriter and should never be taken for granted.

A FICO score is just one of many considerations involved in the evaluation of a borrower's financial strength and creditworthiness. The process of evaluating the borrower's financial strength and creditworthiness is what commercial real estate lenders refer to as "underwriting the borrower." A lender's decision to extend credit to anyone depends on a whole host of factors such as FICO score, net worth, liquidity, debt ratios, mortgage payment history, cash flow, and experience, all of which are discussed in detail in Chapters 3, 4, and 5.

Property Underwriting

As mentioned earlier in this chapter, the single most compelling reason that any commercial real estate lender is willing to make a loan on a commercial property is that the property generates cash flow, which in turn is used to pay back the loan. It is the responsibility of the lender to verify the rental income and the operating expenses of the property and to ensure the sufficiency of that cash flow to pay back the loan. This process of verification of cash flow is referred to as *property underwriting*. The first step in underwriting a commercial property is to calculate the property's cash flow, which is commonly referred to as *net operating income*, or *NOI*.

Net operating income is the property's cash flow or profit before the payment of any principal and interest (the mortgage payment). Principal and interest or, in some instances, interest-only payments are also referred to as *monthly debt service*. In order to calculate the property's NOI, a commercial real estate lender needs to examine certified copies of the property's rent roll, current and historical income and expense statements (also referred to as the profit-and-loss statements, or P&Ls), leases, real estate tax bills, insurance certificates, utility bills, and expense reimbursement records. Depending on the type of property, there may be several other types of financial documents needed to calculate the property's NOI; the ones previously mentioned are considered more than adequate for most property types.

NOI Analysis

Net operating income or NOI analysis begins with an examination of the property's rent roll. A property rent roll is a list of every tenant currently occupying the property and includes a summary of each tenant's name, actual monthly rent, move-in date, lease expiration date, and security deposit, among other things. A property rent roll also indicates the number of vacant units, suites, tenant spaces, or square feet within the property, from which an overall vacancy ratio can be calculated. A typical apartment rent roll includes at minimum the following information:

- ➤ Suite or unit number
- ➤ Tenant name
- ➤ Unit type (i.e., one-bedroom/one-bath unit)
- ➤ Unit or suite size (in square feet)
- ➤ Market rental rate
- ➤ Contract rental rate
- ➤ Lease start date or move-in date
- ➤ Lease expiration date
- ➤ Security deposit

Rent rolls for nonresidential commercial properties, such as retail centers and office and industrial buildings, are slightly different because of the commercial nature of these properties. For example, a typical retail or office rent roll will include at minimum the following details:

- ➤ Suite or unit number
- ➤ Tenant name
- ➤ Suite size (in square feet)
- ➤ Monthly base rent
- ➤ Annual base per square feet (PSF)
- ➤ Monthly CAM reimbursements
- ➤ Monthly real estate tax reimbursements
- ➤ Monthly insurance reimbursements
- ➤ Move-in date and lease expiration date
- ➤ Expense stops
- ➤ Security deposit

The rent roll is a quick way for the lender to calculate the total monthly or annual rental income, referred to as *gross potential income (GPI)*. The phrase "Gross Potential" implies a hypothetical situation. The hypothetical situation we are referring to is concerning occupancy. In other words, gross potential income is the maximum income that can be generated based on an occupancy rate of 100 percent. GPI should, if correctly calculated, equal the sum total of actual rents on all occupied units plus market or asking rents for all vacant units (if there are any vacant units). If there are no vacant units, then GPI is the sum total of actual rents on all the occupied units.

After calculating the GPI, the lender must apply a *vacancy factor* of at least 5 percent or higher. The term "vacancy factor" is the relationship or ratio between the occupied units or the occupied square feet and the property's total rentable units or square feet. For example, if a 200-unit apartment complex has 20 vacant units, then the vacancy ratio or factor is 10 percent (20 ÷ 200 = 0.10 or 10%). If a 50,000-square-foot retail center has 2,500 vacant square feet, then the vacancy ratio or factor is 5 percent (2,500 ÷ 50,000 = 0.05 or 5%). GPI less the vacancy factor results in a net rental income, referred to as *effective gross income*, or *EGI*. EGI is nothing more than gross potential income less the vacancy factor plus *other income*. Other income includes, for example, miscellaneous income collected from application fees, late fees, laundry income, and forfeited security deposits.

The next process in analyzing the property's NOI is to verify all operating expenses. Verifying operating expenses involves reviewing financial statements, often referred to as *profit and loss statements*, or *P&Ls*. Typical operating expenses include real estate taxes, insurance, utilities, repairs and maintenance, cleaning, supplies, landscaping and lawn care, legal and professional services, administrative services, management fees, marketing fees, and capital improvements. These recurring operating expenses are subtracted from the EGI, resulting in the property's NOI. Figure 1-1 is an example of a P&L statement for an apartment complex (multifamily property) that details the calculation of the property's NOI.

As illustrated in Figure 1-1, the property's effective gross income (EGI) and operating expenses yield an annual NOI of $100,000. This NOI, which will be used to pay the mortgage, is the annual cash flow generated from the operation of the property. Net operating income (NOI) is sometimes referred to as *cash flow available for debt service (CFADS)*. As previously mentioned, monthly debt service is the same as the monthly P&I payment. The next step in commercial mortgage underwriting involves calculating the *debt service coverage ratio (DCR)* and estimating the property's *market value*.

Capitalized Value

As demonstrated in Figure 1-1, this income-producing commercial property, which in this example is an apartment complex, generates an annual net operating income or NOI of $100,000. Now it's time to capitalize the NOI in order to calculate the property's *capitalized value*. We do this by dividing the NOI by a market capitalization rate,

Figure 1-1. Profit-and-Loss Statement.

		Annual
Purchase Price $1,000,000		
Gross Potential Rent (GPI)		$250,000
LESS:Vacancy	10%	($25,000)
Effective Gross Income (EGI)		$225,000
OPERATING EXPENSES		
Real Estate Taxes		$40,000
Insurance		$15,000
Repairs & Maintenance		$5,000
Landscaping & Lawn Care		$5,000
Cleaning		$25,000
Pool		$6,000
Utilities		$4,000
Management Fee		$10,000
G&A		$5,000
Replacement Reserves		$10,000
TOTAL EXPENSES		$125,000
Net Operating Income (NOI)		$100,000
LESS:		
Annual Debt Service or Annual P&I Payment*		$80,000
Debt Service Coverage Ratio (DCR)		1.25
Cash Flow Available After Debt Service		$20,000

* The Annual Debt Service is the monthly P&I payment multiplied by twelve months. The monthly P&I payment is based on an $800,000 loan amortized 30 years at an interest rate of 9.40%.

which is a process referred to as *capitalization*. "Capitalized value" in one sense is just another way of saying "market value." You will often hear a lender ask, "What is the capitalized value?" A capitalized value is a value specifically derived using the property's income, which is the reason a lender uses that term from time to time instead of "market value." This method of valuation is referred to by appraisers as the *income approach*. The term *capitalization rate*, on the other hand, is just another way of referring to annual return on capital.

The best way to explain the concept of capitalization is by speaking in terms of rate of return. The term "rate of return" refers to the percentage rate that investors expect to receive on their money. For example, a 10 percent annual rate of return means that the investor expects to receive $10,000 in return for investing $100,000. Annual rates of returns for commercial investment properties can range from a low of 5 percent to as high as 25 percent. However, for the average apartment investor, the standard rate of return or capitalization rate is about 10 percent. If an investor expects to receive a 10 percent annual return on his investment and this investor knows that the property generates net operating income of $100,000 annually, then it stands to reason that this $100,000 represents 10 percent of some value. In other words, this value is the maximum price that an investor is willing to pay in order to achieve this 10 percent rate of return.

By now, you may be asking, "What is the maximum value that will yield a 10 percent annual return?" In order to answer that question, all that is required is to divide the NOI of $100,000 by the rate of return or capitalization rate of 10 percent ($100,000 ÷ 0.10 = $1,000,000). This method of valuation results in a capitalized value of $1 million and therefore represents that maximum value or price an investor would pay based on a 10 percent annual return. The reason the term "capitalization" is used in "capitalization rate" instead of the phrase "rate of return" is that it relates to the amount of capital (money) that one must invest in order to receive a 10 percent return. If an investor desires only a 9 percent rate of return, then that same $100,000 is divided by 9 percent, thus increasing the capitalized value to $1,111,111. A lower capitalization rate means the investor is willing to pay more than $1 million for the property. As the capitalization rate decreases, the capitalized value increases. The opposite effect also holds true; if the capitalization rate increases, the capitalized value decreases.

The capitalized or market value for the property illustrated in Figure 1-1 is calculated the same way. We simply divide the property's annual NOI of $100,000 by the capitalized rate of 10 percent. The estimated market value in this example is $1 million. Now that we have established the market value for the property illustrated in Figure 1-1, it's time to calculate the loan amount. Calculating the maximum loan amount is pretty straight forward. If the lender's maximum LTV is 80 percent, then the maximum loan will be $800,000 ($1,000,000 × .80 = $800,000). The next step is to calculate the actual debt service coverage ratio using the annual debt service payment shown in Figure 1-1.

Debt Service Coverage Ratio

The *debt service coverage ratio,* or *DCR*, is simply a percentage of the property's net operating income (NOI) that exceeds the property's *annual debt service*. For example, if the DCR is 1.25, it signals to the lender that the annual NOI or annual cash flow effectively exceeds the annual debt service by 25 percent. Annual debt service is calculated by multiplying monthly principal and interest payments by twelve. The phrase "annual debt service" is lender slang for twelve months of P&I payments. Calculating the DCR is quite easy; all you have to do is divide the property's NOI by the annual debt service. As illustrated in Figure 1-1, dividing the property's annual NOI of

$100,000 by the annual debt service of $80,000 results in a DCR of 1.25 ($100,000 ÷ $80,000 = 1.25). The property's annual cash flow in this example is 1.25 times greater than the annual debt service. This ratio illustrated in Figure 1-1 is essentially telling the lender that for every dollar of debt service there is $1.25 of net operating income.

The DCR is the standard benchmark used by all lenders in sizing a commercial real estate loan. The minimum DCR for most commercial properties is 1.25. Prior to the financial crisis that began in 2008, debt service coverage ratios for stabilized class A properties dropped as low as 1.10, which was considered very aggressive even during that time.

It is also interesting to note that if the DCR is predetermined, such as 1.25, and if you know the annual debt service based on a desired loan amount, you can effectively calculate the minimum NOI required to service the loan. For example, assume that you wanted to borrow $800,000 and the estimated annual debt service is $80,000. If the lender's minimum DCR is 1.25, how much NOI would be necessary to support the loan? The answer can be calculated by multiplying the annual debt service payment by 1.25 ($80,000 x 1.25 = $100,000). Conversely, if you know the NOI and the minimum DCR is 1.25, you can effectively calculate the maximum annual debt service by dividing the NOI by 1.25 ($100,000 ÷ 1.25 = $80,000). A limit on the annual debt service, in turn, puts a limit on loan amount. When you are using an annual NOI, be sure to use an annual debt service figure as well; if the NOI is monthly, be sure to use a monthly debt service payment. The purpose and theory behind the DCR is to let the lender know whether the property's cash flow is sufficient to service the debt. Minimum DCRs can be as little as 1.05 and as high as 1.50, depending on the property type and the LTV. The minimum DCR is dictated by each lender and is used in pricing the interest rate on every loan.

Final Underwriting Analysis

In Figure 1-1, the calculation of the property's NOI, capitalized value, and DCR is generally all that is needed by a commercial real estate lender to complete the property underwriting exercise. There are two constraints that a lender must use in determining the maximum loan amount. The most notable and easiest to understand is the LTV. However, the lender must first calculate the property's value. As previously discussed, the maximum loan amount for a purchase loan is the lower of 80 percent of purchase price or market value. If the lender calculates a higher market value (the capitalized value), there will be no problem in lending 80 percent of the purchase price. However, if the market value is lower than the purchase price, the borrower will need to put more money down. This particular LTV constraint is unique to purchase loans because of the two competing values. A refinance involves only one estimated value, unless the lender decides to use two values, one estimated in-house and one estimated by an independent appraiser. As demonstrated in Figure 1-1, market value is estimated to be $1 million, which is equal to the purchase price of $1 million. Since there's no difference between the market value and the purchase price, the lender will lend the full $800,000 ($1,000,000 × .80 = $800,000). The other constraint on the maximum loan amount is the DCR. For apartment complexes, the minimum DCR is 1.25. This means the annual NOI must exceed the annual debt service by 25 percent. As demonstrated in Figure 1-1, the annual NOI of $100,000 exceeds the annual debt service by $20,000 or 25 percent and therefore meets the minimum DCR requirement of 1.25 ($100,000 ÷ $80,000 = 1.25). Based on the forgoing analysis, both underwriting constraints fall within the limits set by the lender and will result in the approval of an $800,000 apartment loan.

Notes

1. Wikipedia.org (www.wikipedia.org): Commercial Mortgage.
2. Law.com (www.law.com) (Law Dictionary).
3. R. Kratovil and R. Werner, *Real Estate Law, 9th Edition* (Upper Saddle River, N.J.: Prentice-Hall), Sec 20.09.
4. Dictionary.com (www.dictionary.com): Lien.
5. Kratovil and Werner, Sec 20.09(b).
6. Wikipedia.org (www.wikipedia.org): Mortgage.
7. *Wall Street Journal*, "Money & Investing," p. C12.
8. *Wall Street Journal*, "Money & Investing," p. C12.
9. FICO is an acronym for Fair Isaac Corporation, a leading provider of credit scoring, decision management, fraud detection, and credit risk score services.

CHAPTER 2

PREPARING THE LOAN REQUEST PACKAGE

In Chapter 1, we presented an overview of commercial real estate mortgages, commercial properties, commercial lenders, loan terms, and underwriting, but now you're probably wondering how to make this information work for you or how to put this information to use. Perhaps you have been mulling over an investment opportunity or one of your clients has indicated an interest in purchasing a commercial property. Most likely, either transaction would need commercial financing. If you find yourself in one of these situations, you may feel that it's time to call the lender. Before you do that, can you honestly answer this question: Are you prepared? Can you describe the property, do you know when it was built, when was the property purchased and what was the purchase price, how about the tenants, when do the leases expire, what's the annual net operating income? These and many more are questions the lender will throw your way. The moment you start to hesitate or even utter the words "I don't know," the lender will lose interest and simply end the conversation with the simple suggestion "Why don't you just send me your *loan request package* and I'll look it over." But until you do, you will likely not get very far with that lender. You ask, "What's a loan request package?" This chapter not only answers that question but shows you precisely how to create, organize, and format one into a professional presentation sure to catch the attention of any lender.

Simply filling out and submitting a bank's loan application is usually about as useful as trying to put your resumé on the back of your business card. The truth of the matter is that a typical two-page loan application is nothing more than a sketch of the borrower and transaction.

Then, why do lenders ask for borrowers to complete their loan application? The simple answer is that banks must comply with federal and state regulations. Loan applications are merely formal loan requests (usually on a standard bank form), which are archived in the bank's records for compliance purposes. There are many details that a loan application cannot convey and loan officers know that. A loan application alone is never a substitute for a loan request package. Lenders essentially need more information that only a full loan request package can offer. The quantity and quality of the information directly impacts a lender's credit decision. Credit decisions are developed in phases. The first phase involves a review of the loan application and loan request package. If the information in the loan request package is satisfactory and meets the lender's minimum requirements, the lender will issue a *term sheet* or *letter of interest*. A lender's term sheet, letter of interest, or *letter of intent* (LOI) is nothing more than a two- to three-page preliminary loan proposal outlining the terms of the loan. An LOI is not a commitment to fund the loan; it is merely a conditional proposal subject to underwriting and approval by the loan committee. Remember, basic information found on a loan application such as the borrower's name, address, phone number, employer, income, and basic property information is never enough and should always be supplemented with a complete loan request package. A loan request package is similar to a business plan and highlights the salient facts of the loan transaction. A standard commercial *loan request package* is divided into six sections with the following headings:

1. Executive Summary
2. Property Description
3. Location and Demographics
4. Property Economics
5. Market & Submarket Data
6. Sponsorship

Executive Summary

The first section of the loan request package is the *executive summary*, which is a two- or three-page summary of all of the parts of the entire package; the remaining sections contain the supporting material that the executive summary has highlighted. The executive summary is really the heart and soul of the loan request package and is the first section the lender will read. Whenever a lender needs more details about a certain fact presented in the executive summary, he or she can simply refer to the relevant supporting section at a later time.

An executive summary is an abbreviated narrative or list of all of the salient facts about the loan request, the property, and the borrower. It is much more detailed than the loan application but is brief enough that a loan officer can quickly make a decision about whether the bank is interested in making the loan. The idea is to provide as

much relevant information as possible without boring the loan officer with useless information. Loan officers are inundated with paper-
work and e-mails, and any long-winded presentation will most likely
be pushed aside for some other, less troublesome loan request. Too
much useless information is ordinarily not the problem; it's the lack
of relevant and meaningful information that hamstrings the lender.
A lender in such a situation has no choice but to mothball the
request. If you're lucky, the lender may call you and ask for more
information; without it, the lender won't take the request seriously. A
good executive summary contains only the pertinent information in
an easy-to-read and convenient layout. The outline or layout of an
executive summary is composed of five parts in the following order:

1. Purpose of Loan Request
2. Sources and Uses
3. Property Description and Location
4. Financial Summary
5. Borrower

The amount of information and the degree of detail in each of these
parts varies with the complexity of the transaction, though the general rule of thumb is to be as succinct as possible. Each of these five
parts is discuss in detail in the following sections.

Purpose of Loan Request

The first thing the lender must see in the executive summary is a
clear statement describing the purpose of the loan. Commercial real
estate loans are primarily used to purchase, refinance, or construct
commercial properties. (There are also several other hybrid financing structures that are less familiar, such as loans for
renovations, forward commitments, construction-to-perm, mezza-

nine, sale/leaseback, and participations.) A fourth type of commonly requested loan is a *bridge loan*. The term "bridge loan" refers to a temporary or interim loan usually lasting only a year or two. Bridge loans help borrowers finance properties that need significant repairs or have high vacancies. Properties such as these are considered unstabilized and usually do not qualify for long-term fixed rate financing offered by permanent lenders. Unlike permanent long-term fixed-rate loans, bridge loans are specifically designed to finance both stabilized and unstabilized properties. Bridge loans do not necessarily involve rehabilitation or renovation of the property; therefore, it's important not to confuse bridge loans with rehab or renovation loans. By default, a rehab loan is a bridge loan, but a bridge loan is not always a renovation loan. Bridge loans are requested for many reasons and should be viewed as nothing more than a temporary loan until the goal or objective is accomplished.

Once the loan type has been clearly defined, a subset of questions arises. For example, if the loan is to refinance a project, a lender may wonder why the borrower needs to refinance. Is it to obtain a lower rate? Is it because the original loan term has matured and the borrower needs to pay off the old lender and find a new lender? Is it to pull some cash out? Is it to change the amortization period? Is it a combination of all of these reasons? How about a purchase loan, a bridge loan, or even a construction loan? Do you know how much information is enough or what the lender will ask? The short answer to these questions can be found in the following list of details and queries grouped according to loan type. This list represents just a sample of the various details you should include in the Purpose of Loan Request section, including questions a lender may ask.

1. Purchase loans
   Purchase price

Loan amount

Loan-to-value ratio

Loan term (3, 5, 7, or 10 years)

Amortization (20, 25, or 30 years)

Anticipated interest rate

Payment type: P&I or interest-only

Secondary financing

Purpose of acquisition: Long-term hold or to flip

Rehab needed?

Any repairs or deferred maintenance to cure?

Will the property be renovated and repositioned to create value?

Will the property be converted from an apartment to a condominium?

Will the loan include an earn-out?

2. Refinance loans

Purpose of refinance

Is it to lower the interest rate?

Cash out?

Is it to lengthen the amortization period?

Replace a maturing existing loan?

Buy out existing partners?

Date of purchase

Original purchase price

Cost of any capital improvements or renovations

Existing loan amount

Current value

Purpose of the cash-out dollars

Amount of existing equity

Amount of original equity

Loan payment history

3. Bridge loans

Purpose of bridge

Reposition the property and create value?

Remodel, repair, or renovate?

Convert the use or add more square feet or units?

Raise rents and stabilize occupancy?

Pay for tenant improvements and leasing commissions?

Replace old tenants with new tenants?

Provide more time to sell the property?

Provide for interest reserves?

Will the bridge loan need to convert into a mini-perm?

Is the borrower requesting an earn-out?

What is the exit strategy?

4. Construction loans

Purchase price or cost of the land

Is the land owned free and clear?

Date of land purchase

Zoning

Entitlements

Capital (construction) budget

Loan-to-cost (LTC)

As-completed stabilized value

Name of the general contractor

Name of the architect

Does the developer have city permits?

Are the Plans approved by the city?

Is the site platted or engineered?

Is the developer planning to sell or to hold as a long-term investment?

Is the project preleased?

How will the construction loan be paid off?

You will notice that each loan type includes either a detail or question concerning the history of the property, such as original purchase price or purchase date. The operative word here is "history." A lender loves history. The more you know about the history of the existing loan, the history of the property, and the history of the borrower, the easier it is for the lender to make a credit decision. Also, the more the lender knows about the existing loan or the purpose of the loan, the more creative the lender can be in placing the loan into the right loan program. What about the future? What is the borrower's investment objective? Is the borrower a merchant builder or a long-term investor who plans on holding the property for a very long time? For example, if the borrower plans to sell the property in two years, the lender may structure the loan with easier prepayment terms. Many times the borrower already knows what he is looking for, but it is incumbent on the mortgage broker or the person requesting the loan to clearly communicate the desires of the borrower. Otherwise, both the lender and the borrower will have wasted time, since neither of them understands the other's expectations.

This section of the executive summary should also contain a short *wish list* of desired loan terms such as a percent interest rate, a five-year loan term, 30-year amortization, easy pre-payment, and any special requests, such as interest-only payments or nonrecourse financing. The wish list essentially conveys to the lender the borrower's expectations. What a borrower desires and what a lender can offer are two different things. If the expectations of the borrower are unrealistic the lender will simply take a pass.

Sources and Uses

Now that the lender has a clear picture of what the borrower is looking for and why, it is always best to recap the Purpose of Loan Request section by including a *Schedule of Sources and Uses*. This schedule is very much like a balance sheet; total sources must equal total uses. The schedule is separated into two sections beginning with a list of sources and ending with a list of uses. The most obvious and primary source of funds will always be the lender's loan, which is placed at the top of the list. The second primary source of funds is usually the borrower's cash down payment. Secondary sources might include a second lien, a seller note, or cash sitting in a 1031 Tax Exchange account. The list of sources of funds is generally short, maybe two to three different sources.

The list of uses is usually longer depending on the complexity of the transaction. As illustrated in Figure 2-1, a refinance involving a major renovation, buy-out of a partner, and earn-out necessitates an assortment of uses of the funds. A simple purchase, on the other hand, requires only a single use of the funds. The list of uses tells the lender unequivocally what the loan will be used for and how the money will be spent. Uses must be explicit. For example, part of the loan will include cash-out to the borrower, but simply stating that there is $100,000 cash-out to the borrower is not sufficient. A lender wants to know why the borrower needs that much cash-out. Is it to recover rehab costs, buy out a partner, make improvements, pay down other debts, or purchase another property? Other uses can include tenant improvements and leasing commissions, broker fees, lender fees, financing costs, prepayment penalties, legal fees, title fees, or earn-outs. Figure 2-1 is an example of a typical schedule of Sources and Uses of Funds for both a purchase and a refinance.

Property Description and Location

The executive summary should also include a very *brief description of the property and its location*. As previously mentioned, the loan

Figure 2-1. Schedule of Sources and Uses.

Purchase		
Sources of Funds		
1st Lien Mortgage	$2,000,000	80%
2nd Lien (Seller Financing or Private Lender)	$125,000	5%
Equity (Borrower's Cash Down Payment)	<u>$375,000</u>	<u>15%</u>
TOTAL SOURCES	$2,500,000	100%
Uses of Funds		
Purchase of a 50-Unit Apartment Complex	$2,500,000	100%
TOTAL USES	$2,500,000	

Refinance		
Sources of Funds		
1st Lien Mortgage	$5,000,000	100%
TOTAL SOURCES	$5,000,000	100%
Uses of Funds		
Pay Off Existing Loan	$3,000,000	60%
Renovations and Rehab Costs	$1,000,000	20%
Buy Out a Partner	$100,000	2%
Mortgage Broker Fee	$50,000	1%
Lender Fee	$50,000	1%
Appraisal, Phase I and Structural Report	$10,000	0%
Refinancing Costs	$30,000	1%
Legal Fees	$20,000	0%
Title, Survey, and Escrows	$40,000	1%
Earn-out	<u>$700,000</u>	<u>14%</u>
TOTAL USES	$5,000,000	100%

request package itself has a complete section dedicated to the property description and one for the property's location and demographics, so it's not necessary to go into too much detail here. The objective of the executive summary is just to highlight key characteristics of both the property and its location. The following list is a sample of basic property information grouped according to property type most often highlighted in an executive summary:

Apartments

Name of the project

Physical address

Brief description of location (e.g., located in west Houston near Beltway & I-10)

Number of units and net rentable area

Occupancy

Year built/year renovated

Construction type: walk-up garden, midrise, high-rise

Type of parking: covered, multilevel garage, subterranean

Utilities paid by landlord

Utilities paid by tenant

Retail

Name of the project

Physical address

Brief description of location (e.g., located in north Houston near The Woodlands)

Type of retail: strip center, grocery-anchored center, neighborhood center, mall

Net rentable square feet (NRA)

Number of tenants

Occupancy

Year built/year renovated

List of anchor tenants, including national and regional tenants like Blockbuster Video

Type of leases (e.g., triple net or modified gross)

Office

Name of the project

Physical address

Brief description of location (e.g., located in south Houston)

Type of office (downtown or suburban; high-rise, suburban midrise, medical)

Net rentable square feet (NRA)

List of tenants occupying more than 20% of the building

Occupancy

Year built/year renovated

List of major tenants, including national and regional or publicly traded companies

Type of leases (e.g., full service or gross, modified gross, or triple net-NNN)

Industrial

Name of the project

Physical address

Brief description of location (e.g., located in east Houston)

Type of industrial (e.g., office/warehouse, R&D, light industrial, bulk distribution)

Net rentable square feet (NRA)

Number of tenants

Occupancy

Year built/year renovated

List of major tenants, including national and regional or publicly traded companies

Type of leases (e.g., full service or gross, modified gross, or triple net-NNN)

Number of truck bays, type of rail service area

Ceiling height

Parking spaces

Percentage of office finish-out to warehouse space

Percentage of air-conditioned warehouse space

Financial Summary

The *financial summary* section of the executive summary features key economic data found in the Property Economics section of the loan request package such as purchase price, loan-to-value, annual NOI, annual operating expenses, debt coverage ratio, and average rent per square foot. As previously mentioned at the beginning of this chapter, the loan request package itself has a complete section dedicated to property economics cash flow, and loan analysis, so it's not necessary to include full page rent rolls, cash flow schedules, or financial statements. The goal here is to underscore key financial statistics for easy reference. The following list is a sample of key financial data most often highlighted in an executive summary:

- ➤ Purchase price
- ➤ Purchase price per unit (apartments) or per SF (commercial)
- ➤ Average rent per SF per year (commercial)
- ➤ Average rent per month per unit (apartments)
- ➤ Gross Potential Rental Income (GPI)
- ➤ Triple net recoveries or utility expense reimbursements
- ➤ Other or miscellaneous income
- ➤ Actual vacancy rate
- ➤ Market vacancy rate

> ➤ Effective gross income (EGI)
> ➤ Operating expenses (both fixed and variable)
> ➤ Net operating income (NOI)
> ➤ Monthly or annual proposed P&I payment
> ➤ Debt service coverage ratio (DCR)
> ➤ Combined debt service coverage ratio (CDCR)
> ➤ Loan-to-value ratio (LTV)
> ➤ Loan-to-cost ratio (LTC)

Borrower

The last part of the executive summary is a *brief description of the borrower* or *borrowers* and the *key principals*, namely the *guarantors*. It's best to start off listing the name of the actual borrowing entity. A borrowing entity can be a company or a legal entity such as a limited partnership, a limited liability company, or a corporation. The borrower can also be a single individual or multiple individuals called co-borrowers. It is important to summarize how title will be vested and to include a list of each co-owner or key principal by name. The phrase "key principal" is another term for "guarantor." If the borrower is an individual or group of individuals, it is assumed that they will also be the guarantors. This type of ownership structure is easily understood by the lender. However, whenever there is a legal entity involving general partners, limited partners and managing members, it can get complicated. General partners and managing members must be identified. It's also important to identify limited partners and nonmanaging members who have greater than a 20 percent ownership interest in the property. Unless the loan is a nonrecourse loan, general partners and managing members must guarantee the loan, which makes them guarantors. However, there are occasions when an additional guarantor is needed, so be sure to identify them, as well.

Property Description

The *property description* section of the loan request package is where a lender can find a complete physical description of the land and all of the improvements, including visual aids such as photos, site plans, floor plans, building plans, surveys, and aerials. Unlike the executive summary, which highlights basic property information (e.g., address, property type, number of units, square footage [SF], age), this section is more descriptive. Property and site details such as lot size, site and building amenities, zoning, recent renovations, planned renovations, construction details, anchor tenants, gross building square feet, and net rentable square feet should all be thoroughly covered in this section. Gross building square feet is the size of the building measured from the surface or face of the exterior walls, whereas net rentable square feet is the total of all usable air-conditioned interior space. Net rentable square feet can be found in either the rent roll or leases. There is no right or wrong way to prepare this section, but what is important is to list as much information and to describe the property as fully as possible. Experience and time are the best teachers as to the type and quantity of information one should include in this section. Since there are many different types of properties, it would be difficult to list each and every physical component of each property type, but a general rule is to think like a buyer. A buyer would not purchase without first inspecting the property and neither would a lender, so try to be as descriptive as possible concerning the building components. The lender may have to foreclose on the property someday and wants to know everything about the physical condition of the collateral, as well as the financial condition. Following is a general list of property and site details and visual aids commonly found in the property description section:

Property and Site Details

- Property name and physical address
- Property type (e.g., apartments, retail, office, self-storage miniwarehouse)
- Number of units or total net rentable SF
- Occupancy
- Year built/year renovated, expanded, remodeled
- Number of tenants
- Average apartment unit size in SF or average tenant space size in SF
- List of anchor tenants (e.g., the grocer anchor in a retail shopping center)
- List of tenants occupying more than 20% of the total space
- Site/land details
  - Purchase price
  - Total SF or acreage
  - Shape, layout, and general dimensions
  - Zoning
  - Ingress and egress
  - Visibility and signage
  - Utilities
  - Easements or deed restrictions
  - Roads and shared driveways
  - Excess land
- Construction details
  - Configuration, design features, functional utility
  - Number of buildings
  - Building height (number of stories)
  - Type of roof (flat, pitched)
  - Foundation
  - Mechanical and electrical systems
  - Type of heating and air-conditioning systems
  - Public utilities

Number of elevators

Number of bay doors (grade level, dock high)

Ceiling height

Type of exterior wall (e.g., brick, concrete tilt-up wall, wood siding)

Type of parking (garage, open lot, number of spaces)

Parking ratio per 1,000 SF or per unit (apartments)

Deferred maintenance or needed repairs

Visual Aids

- ➤ Photographs of the property and site
- ➤ Photographs of adjacent properties and bordering streets and neighborhood
- ➤ Site plan, survey, or recorded plat
- ➤ Floor plans
- ➤ Stacking plan (office buildings only)
- ➤ Aerial photographs
- ➤ Construction elevations/drawings

Location and Demographics

The *Location and Demographics* section of the loan request package allows the lender to determine the exact location of the property. It also includes general demographic information such as population estimates, unemployment rates, and median household income. It's best to start with the physical address, followed by a brief description of the neighborhood and immediate vicinity (preferably within a range of three miles). For example, after providing the physical address of a Starbucks, located at 2050 W. Gray, Houston, Texas 77019, you might add a comment indicating that this particular Starbucks is located in the trendy River Oaks Shopping Center just four miles west of downtown. If the prospective lender is not from Houston, there's no way the lender would ever know that this particular corner is a high-end retail destination located in the affluent section of Houston called River Oaks. There's no doubt a local lender would know that, but don't assume that other lenders will. Loan request packages are routinely duplicated and sent to dozens of national lenders who are unfamiliar with most submarkets. The description of the immediate vicinity should include a list of adjacent properties, names of bordering streets, nearby major thoroughfares, and landmarks or major retail stores. Other items of interest to the lender might be the distance in blocks or miles from a major employment center, shopping center, mall, university, or hospital. Listing names of regional and national retailers is significant because it signals to the lender that the property is located in a part of town that is thriving and where, it is hoped, property values are rising, too. If there are residential single-family homes in the area, comment on the average price or range of values and age of construction. A lender may also want to know if there is new construction in the area and whether the employment rate is trending up or down. If applicable, be sure to explain that the property is located in an older, established area of town where new commercial developments are replacing older commercial properties.

Along with the narrative description of the location, it is extremely important to include several maps within this section. Following is a list of the type of maps and other helpful visual aids that are extremely useful to the lender:

> ➤ Local map (if using Yahoo or Google Maps, zoom in close enough for a scale of approximately 1 inch for every 1,000 feet)
> ➤ Area map (zoom out until there is about a three-mile radius from the center of the subject property)
> ➤ Regional map (usually a city map)

- ➤ Aerial photographs
- ➤ Demographic statistical information for a one-, three-, and five-mile radius of the subject property. Such statistical information can be found on U.S. Census Web sites and includes the following:

> Population
>
> Per capita income
>
> Median income
>
> Average household income
>
> Average household size
>
> Average home value
>
> Percentage of owner-occupied households
>
> Percentage of non-owner-occupied households (renters)
>
> Employment statistics
>
> Vehicular traffic counts
>
> Population density
>
> Schools, colleges, and universities

Property Economics

A thorough and comprehensive *Property Economics* section serves as the backbone of any noteworthy loan request package. No loan request package is ever complete without the Property Economics section, so pay close attention to this part of the chapter. This section is where the lender can find a complete analysis of the loan and the current and historical cash flow. At times, this section is merely stuffed with a rent roll and a two-page financial statement. Depending on the type of property and the type of loan, it's probable, if not certain, that you will need more than that. A first-class property economic section should include a unit-mix and rent schedule, a schedule of income, a summary of historical cash flow, a pro forma cash flow statement, a loan analysis, and supporting financial documents. Most of these are one-page summaries, which are prepared by the commercial mortgage broker, the broker's analyst, or even the borrower if he or she happens to be good at financial analysis. A description and sample of these are discussed at the end of this section, but first we must say a few words about the discipline and art of financial analysis and financial statements in general.

Financial Statements

When the phrase "financial statement" is used in connection with the property economic section, it is referring to the property's *income and expense statement* or the *profit-and-loss statement* (P&L), not the borrower's personal financial statement. Financial analysis begins with a review of both income and expenses, which must be explained in detail, including any anomalies or nonrecurring expenditures that were excluded from the analysis. Financial statements vary widely both in format and in frequency. For example, there may be monthly or annual statements, as well as computer-generated or manually prepared statements. What matters most is that the financial statements be consistent and complete. If the statements are prepared monthly, be sure to include all twelve calendar months; if they are annual, be sure that the annual statements include all income and expense categories for that year. Partial-year financial statements are essentially useless to a lender, so if you receive a financial statement with fewer than twelve months of income and expenses for any given year, don't bother including it in the loan request package. It is incumbent upon the mortgage broker to review the property financial statements for inconsistencies and completeness before inserting them in the loan request package. If the lender has faulty information, he will cease his review until his questions are answered. Monthly or yearly financial statements don't always present a clear picture of the financial history of the property or provide a true representation of the cash flow. For example, total rental income indicated on the current rent roll, including utility reimbursements, is often inconsistent or contradicts the rental income and utility reimbursements shown on the financial statement. Explanations are often needed to describe inconsistencies in monthly income or expense reimbursements. The same care needs to be applied to the operating expenses. Cash accounting, in contrast to accrual accounting, can skew an annual income and expense statement. For example, real estate taxes, which are usually due or paid in lump sum once a year, may show up twice on the operating statement if they are paid in January and then again in December of the same year. If that happens, real estate taxes will be significantly overstated for that particular year, resulting in a skewed net operating income. This is just one example of the kinds of errors or inconsistencies that need to be explained and footnoted for the lender. A loan officer or analyst who assists the loan officer is usually experienced enough to catch these errors but don't assume that they will. However, if the mortgage broker can catch these sorts of errors and omissions first, it will make it a lot easier on the lender and save a lot of time.

Financial Analysis

The primary purpose of the property economic section is to make the lender's job easier. As previously mentioned, property financial statements can be inconsistent from year to year and often need to be footnoted for inconspicuous omissions and anomalies. In order to prevent the lender from misinterpreting these financial statements, which may lead her to decline the loan, it's best to create a one-page summary of the property's historical income and expenses. Not only will the historical data be consistent and well organized, but they will be presumably free of anomalies, aberrations, omissions, and nonrecurring expenses. This one-page summary is referred to as the property's *historical cash flow*. Other possible titles or headings may be *Historical Income and Expenses* or *Cash Flow Analysis*. No matter what label is assigned to this one-page cash flow summary, it's imperative that annual income and expenses be consistent and easy to follow.

Another purpose of the property economic section is to fully identify all sources of income. It's not enough just to provide historical annual income; lenders will need to know additional details about each and every paying tenant who occupies the building. It is for this reason that a *schedule of income* should be included within this section of the loan request package, preferably on the first page. A schedule of income is sometimes referred to as a *unit-mix and rent schedule*, depending on the property type.

The contents and format of the property economic section depend loosely on the complexity of the transaction and may differ slightly according to the property type. It would be impossible to create a one-size-fits-all template for every loan request and property type; the templates in this chapter are merely recommendations. With this in mind, we have organized the property economics section into four parts that will suit most loan requests and just about any property type. As previously discussed, all sources of income and historical and current income and expenses must be consolidated and organized in an easy-to-follow one-page summary referred to as the *schedule of income* and *historical cash flow*, respectively. The third part of the property economics section, not yet mentioned, is the *loan analysis*, which may also be a single-page summary. The loan analysis includes a combination of *historical* and *underwriting cash flow* used to size the loan. The phrase "sizing the loan" simply means applying certain underwriting assumptions (e.g., a minimum vacancy rate, a fixed management fee, or minimum replacement reserves within the cash flow model) in order to derive an underwriting cash flow, sometimes referred to as the *underwriting NOI*. You can use "Underwriting Cash Flow" instead of "Loan Analysis" as an alternative heading for this one-page summary. Either is acceptable.

The last part of the property economic section should include the supporting documents used in underwriting and analyzing the loan and cash flow, such as the tenant rent roll and profit-and-loss statements provided by the borrower's property manager, accountant, or bookkeeper.

In summary, the property economic section, no matter how complicated the loan transaction may be, should generally be organized in the following order:

- Schedule of Income (1st page)
- Historical Cash Flow (2nd page)
- Loan Analysis (3rd page)
- Supporting documents (rent roll, property financial statements)

Schedule of Income

The *schedule of income* is nothing more than a single-page summary identifying all sources of primary and secondary income. Primary income is the monthly base rent paid by the tenants. Base rent is just another term for "minimum rent" excluding utility reimbursements and other additional monthly charges. Secondary income can come from many sources, such as expense and utility reimbursements, application fees, late fees, returned-check fees, parking fees, laundry and vending revenue, and forfeited security deposits. In order to create a schedule of income, you will need a detailed tenant rent roll and a monthly or annual income and expense statement. Begin with the tenant rent roll and locate the base rent. Secondary sources of income, often referred to as *expense reimbursements* or *miscellaneous income*, can be found on the property's financial statements. However, some of these secondary sources of income may be found in the rent roll alongside the base rent as well, especially on tenant rent rolls prepared by professional management companies using sophisticated computer software. Unlike multifamily tenant rent rolls, commercial tenant rent rolls are often incomplete and provide very little detail regarding secondary-source income, even though these secondary sources of income are evident on the financial statements. Reconciling secondary sources of income on the commercial tenant rent roll and on the financial statement can be a daunting, if not impossible task even for a seasoned underwriter. If you find yourself in this situation, try searching for secondary sources of income such as monthly charges for common-area-maintenance (CAM) and utility reimbursements within the individual leases, though this too may not be practical. You may not have any of the leases and if you do, they are usually too lengthy and convoluted to read. This particular situation is unique to commercial properties. Multifamily tenant rent rolls and their corresponding financial statements are less complicated, making it much easier to identify and summarize both primary and secondary sources of income.

A schedule of income can be presented in many ways, but the decision about which format to use is often left to the discretion of the analyst or the person preparing the loan request package. Essentially, there are only two distinct types of income schedules worth mentioning, which are incidentally the most popular formats among underwriters and analysts. The first is a multifamily schedule of income, most commonly referred to as the *unit mix and rent schedule*. The second is a commercial schedule of income, often referred to simply as a *rent schedule*. The terms "rent schedule" and "unit mix and rent schedule" should not be confused with the term "tenant rent roll." A tenant rent roll is a multipage document prepared and used by the borrower or property management company in operating and managing the property. Though not officially recognized or used by accountants, a tenant rent roll is considered to be just as important as a financial statement. Figure 2-2 is an example of a typical unit mix and rent schedule created from a multifamily tenant rent roll. Multifamily tenant rent rolls vary in length and can range from as few as five tenants listed on one page to as many as a thousand tenants listed in a fifty-page document.

Because multifamily tenant rent rolls can be rather long, it may not be practical to list every individual tenant in the schedule of income. We therefore recommend that a unit mix and rent schedule like the one illustrated in Figure 2-2 be created to provide the lender with a statistical overview of the unit types and rental rates on a single page. Unit mix and rent schedules are actually designed specifically for apartments because of their usual lengthy rent rolls and are rarely ever created or used for commercial properties.

The unit mix and rent schedule illustrated in Figure 2-2 consolidates and groups 240 individual tenants listed on a twelve-page multifamily tenant rent roll into six different types of rental units, hence the term "unit mix." This unit mix and rent schedule, unlike the twelve-page tenant rent roll, provides the lender with a snapshot of

Figure 2-2. Multifamily Schedule of Income.

Unit Mix and Rent Schedule							
Unit Type	No. of Units	SF	Total SF	Unit Rent	Rent Per SF	Monthly Rent	Annual Rent
1BR, 1 Bth	24	813	19,500	$700	$0.86	$16,800	$201,600
2BR, 1 Bth	20	925	18,500	$750	$0.81	$15,000	$180,000
2 BR, 1.5 Bth	88	1,000	88,000	$825	$0.83	$72,600	$871,200
2BR, 2 Bth	32	1,125	36,000	$900	$0.80	$28,800	$345,600
3 BR, 2 Bth	56	1,250	70,000	$975	$0.78	$54,600	$655,200
3 BR, 2.5 Bth	20	1,400	28,000	$1,050	$0.75	$21,000	$252,000
Total/Average	240	1,083	260,000	$870	$0.80	$208,800	$2,505,600

the property's unit mix, including the total number of each unit type, unit square feet, total unit square feet, monthly rent, rent per square foot, total monthly rent, and total annual rent.

A commercial tenant rent roll looks entirely different from a multifamily tenant rent roll and is often used in lieu of a separate schedule of income as demonstrated in the multifamily example. The appearance and format of a commercial schedule of income often varies from property type to property type and usually cannot be created by using a standard template. Often a commercial schedule of income, also referred to simply as a rent schedule, is nothing more than a modified version of the property's tenant rent roll. In other words, the commercial schedule of income will look very much like the actual commercial tenant rent roll provided by the borrower or management company. Figure 2-3 is an example of a commercial schedule of income or rent schedule for a retail shopping center.

Rent schedules for other types of commercial properties, such as office, industrial, and self-storage facilities, are very similar to the retail rent schedule illustrated in Figure 2-3. It should be noted that rent schedules, such as the one illustrated in Figure 2-3, often resemble the actual tenant rent roll prepared by the management company, so why the redundancy? In reality, commercial tenant rent rolls are not that reliable and often omit critical information, such as monthly CAM charges, utility reimbursements, move-in dates, lease expiration dates, and rent concessions. Reconstructing a commercial rent schedule ensures that the lender has been given information that is both up-to-date and accurate. A commercial rent schedule of this type is extremely useful, if not invaluable, and provides the lender with a single source for critical data such as move-in and lease expiration dates, monthly CAM charges, expense reimbursements, vacancy and occupancy ratios, rental rates, and monthly and annual totals. When creating a commercial rent schedule, be sure to use the number and type of column headings shown in Figure 2-3, if at all

Figure 2-3. Commercial Schedule of Income.

Retail Center Rent Schedule

Suite	Tenant	SF	% Space	Move-In Date	Lease Expiration	Monthly Rent	Rent PSF	MONTHLY REIMBURSEMENTS			Total Monthly Income	Annual Income
								Taxes	Insurance	CAM		
A	AllState Insurance	3,000	12.0%	1-Jun-00	6-May-05	$2,500	$10.00	$350	$150	$250	$3,250	$39,000
B	H&R Block	3,300	13.2%	30-Apr-02	4-Apr-07	$2,544	$9.25	$375	$170	$275	$3,364	$40,365
C	Game Stop	1,400	5.6%	1-May-05	5-Apr-10	$1,108	$9.50	$175	$100	$150	$1,533	$18,400
D	Dollar Store	2,800	11.2%	1-Jul-03	4-Jun-08	$2,217	$9.50	$325	$150	$225	$2,917	$35,000
E	Hair Salon	3,500	14.0%	30-Jan-01	4-Jan-06	$2,771	$9.50	$325	$200	$280	$3,576	$42,910
F	Dry Cleaners	3,000	12.0%	30-Jun-06	4-Jun-11	$2,375	$9.50	$325	$150	$250	$3,100	$37,200
G	Hallmark Cards	1,500	6.0%	1-Aug-99	5-Jul-04	$1,125	$9.00	$175	$100	$120	$1,520	$18,240
H	Subway	3,200	12.8%	1-Jan-04	5-Dec-08	$2,533	$9.50	$375	$175	$250	$3,333	$40,000
I	Radio Shack	1,800	7.2%	1-Aug-00	6-Jul-05	$1,350	$9.00	$200	$100	$150	$1,800	$21,600
J	Vacant	1,500	6.0%	1-Sep-05	6-Aug-10	$1,500	$12.00	$150	$100	$125	$1,875	$22,500
						$20,023	$9.61	$2,775	$1,395	$2,075	$26,268	$315,215

	SF	% Space
Occupied SF	23,500	94.0%
Vacant SF	1,500	6.0%
TOTAL SF	25,000	100.0%

possible. Commercial rent schedules can be customized or presented in many different formats and are not standardized by any means.
No matter which format you choose, be sure that the information
and figures under each of the column headings are clearly articulat-
ed and easy to follow.

Historical Cash Flow

The second part of the property economics section, which immediately follows the schedule of income, is a one-page summary of the
property's *historical cash flow*, preferably for the two most recent full
calendar years and for the current year, referred to as year-to-date
(YTD). For example, if the date of the loan request is July 15, 2009,
the lender will need to examine the year-end 2007, year-end 2008,
and the year-to-date 2009 operating statements. The year-to-date
2009 operating statement will only include the first six months of
2009 ending June 30, 2009. The term "year-end" simply means a
full calendar year running from January through December. "Year-to-
date" refers to a partial year and must specify the ending month. For
example, a partial year or year-to-date column in a cash flow summary must include in the column heading the words "year-to-date
ending June 30" if the property financial statement only represents
the first six months of the year.

   This single-page summary is a reconstruction or consolidation of
approximately three years' worth of operating income and expenses
into a single cash flow statement. However, this presumably simple
task of consolidating three years' worth of financial statements into a
single cash flow summary may not be enough. The real goal here is
to create a tailored and polished version for the lender. With a well-
organized and cleaned-up version of the statements, a lender can
quickly compare and identify both positive and negative trends in net
rental revenue and expenses from year to year without having to

labor through multiple pages of financial documents. The primary purpose of the historical cash flow summary is to aid the lender in spotting unusual operating expenses, nonrecurring capital expenditures, or huge spikes or dips in rental income during the past two to three years. If there is a partial year or year-to-date column within the cash flow summary, a fourth column should be added to represent the annualized cash flow of the partial year. This annualized column is a unique feature not found in property financial statements and is helpful in identifying positive or negative trends in year-to-date cash flow.

The historical cash flow summary is composed of two parts, the income section and the operating expense section. The income section is usually the easier of the two to recreate and contains line items for gross potential income, loss to lease, vacancy, and net rental income, as well as several line items for nonrental income, such as expense and utility reimbursements and miscellaneous income, which is commonly referred to as "other income." The level of detail is usually only as good as what is shown on the actual financial statement. Nevertheless, there's not much modification involved in reconstructing the historical income.

The same does not hold true for operating expenses. Unlike the income section, reconstructing or modifying the operating expense section can be daunting and time consuming. Often you may come across a detailed list of repairs, maintenance, and supplies that consumes multiple pages within the operating expense section of a property financial statement. Professional management companies that use sophisticated software to classify each and every operating expense according to a corresponding ledger account can produce a very tedious and protracted list of fixed and variable expenses. In a situation like this, it's better to use a consolidated version if one can be generated by the software program. If a consolidated version is not available, you may have to manually group these operating expenses into a single expense category such as "utilities" or "repairs and maintenance" in order to condense a three- or four-page income and expense statement into the one-page historical cash flow summary. For example, expense categories such roof repairs, supplies, heating and air conditioning repairs, pool maintenance, landscaping, plumbing, electrical repairs, and painting are all related and can be grouped into a single general expense category called "repairs and maintenance" in order to simplify the presentation and save space. The decision to group operating expenses into broad categories within the summary is a judgment call. An example of a fairly standard one-page historical cash flow summary is illustrated in Figures 2-4, 2-5, and 2-6.

A typical historical cash flow summary includes at least four columns. The first and second column each show a full calendar year's worth of income and expenses. The third column represents the partial year or year-to-date cash flow. The fourth and last column is the annualized cash flow. Though not included in the example illustrated in Figure 2-4, a fifth column is often added to show income and expenses for the trailing twelve months. A *trailing twelve-month cash flow* is an annual total of income and expenses for the preceding twelve consecutive months. For example, if the current date is June 2009, the trailing twelve-month cash flow column would include income and expenses from July 2008 through June 2009.

Loan Analysis

The third part of the property economics section is the analyst's or mortgage broker's *loan analysis*. This underwriting cash flow model, similar to the schedule of income and historical cash flow summary, should be no more than a one-page summary. Other titles or headings for this type of analysis may be "underwriting cash flow," "underwriting NOI," "pro forma cash flow," and "stabilized cash

(text continues on page 78)

Figure 2-4. Historical Cash Flow: Multifamily.

		Jan.-Dec. 2007		Jan.-Dec. 2008		Year-to-date ending June 2009		Annualized 2009
GROSS POTENTIAL INCOME		$2,505,600		$2,600,000		$1,300,000		$2,600,000
Loss to Lease		($150,000)		($100,000)		($35,000)		($70,000)
Gross Rental Income (actual)		$2,355,600		$2,500,000		$1,265,000		$2,530,000
Vacancy & Collection Loss	15%	($350,000)	11%	($265,000)	7%	($90,000)	7%	($180,000)
NET RENTAL INCOME		$2,005,600		$2,235,000		$1,175,000		$2,350,000
OTHER INCOME								
Late Fees		$16,873		$15,000		$5,200		$10,400
Laundry & Vending		$2,052		$2,000		$3,700		$7,400
Application Fees		$7,949		$5,000		$2,900		$5,800
TOTAL		$26,874		$22,000		$11,800		$23,600
EFFECTIVE GROSS INCOME (EGI)		$2,032,474		$2,257,000		$1,186,800		$2,373,600
EXPENSES								
Real Estate Taxes		($250,000)		($275,000)		($145,000)		($290,000)
Insurance		($85,000)		($90,000)		($46,000)		($92,000)
Gas		($74,462)		($75,000)		($34,000)		($68,000)
Water & Sewer		($113,490)		($114,000)		($58,000)		($116,000)
Electric		($20,422)		($22,000)		($12,000)		($24,000)
Trash		($32,341)		($33,000)		($14,600)		($29,200)
Pest Control		($487)		($5,000)		($2,800)		($5,600)
Telephone & Communications		($3,305)		($3,400)		($1,950)		($3,900)
Repairs & Maintenance		($65,000)		($96,000)		($54,000)		($108,000)
Supplies		($4,726)		($14,000)		($10,000)		($20,000)
Cleaning & Make Ready		($16,595)		($20,000)		($25,000)		($50,000)
Landscaping		($13,328)		($14,000)		($12,500)		($25,000)
Salaries		($245,000)		($257,000)		($125,000)		($250,000)
Payroll Taxes		($29,577)		($45,000)		($25,000)		($50,000)
Security		($5,000)		($4,800)		($3,200)		($6,400)
Management Fee		($55,000)		($67,710)		($47,440)		($94,880)
Nonrevenue Units		($8,600)		($12,000)		($7,250)		($14,500)
Legal & Professional		($6,175)		($5,000)		($4,700)		($9,400)
Advertising & Marketing		($15,000)		($18,000)		($5,600)		($11,200)
General & Administrative		($12,152)		($13,000)		($17,760)		($35,520)
Miscellaneous		($14,424)		($10,000)		($5,000)		($10,000)
Replacement Reserves		($85,000)		($125,000)		($30,000)		($60,000)
TOTAL OPERATING EXPENSES		($1,155,084)		($1,318,910)		($686,800)		($1,373,600)
NET OPERATING INCOME (NOI)*		$877,390		$938,090		$500,000		$1,000,000

* Net cash flow before debt service

Figure 2-5. Historical Cash Flow: Office.

		Jan.-Dec. 2007		Jan.-Dec. 2008		Year-to-date ending June 2009		Annualized 2009
GROSS POTENTIAL INCOME		$4,500,000		$4,775,000		$2,550,000		$5,100,000
LESS: Rental Concessions		($100,000)		($75,000)		($32,000)		($64,000)
Gross Rental Income		$4,400,000		$4,700,000		$2,518,000		$5,036,000
Vacancy & Collection Loss	12%	($525,000)	7%	($350,000)	9%	($225,000)	9%	($450,000)
NET RENTAL INCOME		$3,875,000		$4,350,000		$2,293,000		$4,586,000
OTHER INCOME								
Expense Recovery (Base Year Stop)		$47,000		$45,600		$8,990		$17,980
Utility Expense Reimbursements		$18,000		$16,500		$6,500		$13,000
Cell Tower Lease (Roof)		$12,000		$12,500		$7,500		$15,000
Parking Garage Income		$8,500		$9,700		$4,200		$8,400
TOTAL		$85,500		$84,300		$27,190		$54,380
EFFECTIVE GROSS INCOME (EGI)		$3,960,500		$4,434,300		$2,320,190		$4,640,380
EXPENSES								
Property Taxes		($225,000)		($237,000)		($122,648)		($245,295)
Insurance		($75,000)		($73,000)		($37,778)		($75,555)
Electricity		($625,000)		($590,000)		($305,325)		($610,650)
Gas		($75,000)		($65,000)		($33,638)		($67,275)
Water & Sewer		($45,000)		($48,000)		($24,840)		($49,680)
Trash		($45,000)		($37,000)		($19,148)		($38,295)
HVAC Service Contract		($7,500)		($9,500)		($4,916)		($9,833)
Elevator Service Contract		($24,000)		($27,000)		($13,973)		($27,945)
Landscaping		($24,000)		($28,500)		($14,749)		($29,498)
Repair and Maintenance		($250,000)		($267,000)		($138,173)		($276,345)
Janitorial		($125,000)		($129,000)		($66,758)		($133,515)
Window Cleaning		($50,000)		($49,000)		($25,358)		($50,715)
Salaries & Payroll		($120,000)		($130,000)		($67,275)		($134,550)
Security/Life Safety		($25,000)		($27,000)		($13,973)		($27,945)
Telephone & Communications		($7,500)		($8,300)		($4,295)		($8,591)
Parking		($48,000)		($43,500)		($22,511)		($45,023)
Legal & Professional		($15,000)		($14,500)		($7,504)		($15,008)
Management Fee		($158,000)		($149,500)		($77,366)		($154,733)
Marketing		($7,500)		($8,500)		($4,399)		($8,798)
Office & Administrative		($25,000)		($24,700)		($12,782)		($25,565)
Miscellaneous		($50,000)		($26,000)		($13,455)		($26,910)
Replacement Reserves		($62,500)		($76,000)		($39,330)		($78,660)
TOTAL OPERATING EXPENSES		($2,089,000)		($2,068,000)		($1,070,190)		($2,140,380)
NET OPERATING INCOME (NOI)*		$1,871,500		$2,366,300		$1,250,000		$2,500,000

* Net cash flow before debt service

Figure 2-6. Historical Cash Flow: Retail.

		Jan.-Dec. 2007		Jan.-Dec. 2008		Year-to-date ending June 2009		Annualized 2009
GROSS POTENTIAL INCOME		$1,650,000		$1,725,000		$865,000		$1,730,000
Vacancy	14%	($235,000)	11%	($195,000)	8%	($71,500)	8%	($143,000)
NET RENTAL INCOME		$1,415,000		$1,530,000		$793,500		$1,587,000
REIMBURSEMENTS								
Real Estate Taxes		$74,000		$81,000		$43,000		$86,000
Insurance		$18,000		$22,500		$12,500		$25,000
Common Area Maintenance (CAM)		$180,000		$212,000		$110,000		$220,000
Miscellaneous Income		$4,200		$5,000		$3,700		$7,400
TOTAL		$276,200		$320,500		$169,200		$338,400
EFFECTIVE GROSS INCOME (EGI)		$1,691,200		$1,850,500		$962,700		$1,925,400
EXPENSES								
Property Taxes		($87,000)		($91,000)		($47,320)		($94,640)
Insurance		($25,000)		($26,500)		($13,780)		($27,560)
Electricity		($6,000)		($6,500)		($3,380)		($6,760)
Gas		($2,500)		($2,700)		($1,678)		($3,356)
Water & Sewer		($3,000)		($2,800)		($1,456)		($2,912)
Trash		($7,500)		($8,400)		($4,368)		($8,736)
Repair and Maintenance		($50,000)		($52,500)		($26,250)		($52,500)
Landscaping & Grounds		($24,000)		($23,500)		($12,220)		($24,440)
Salaries & Payroll		($50,000)		($51,000)		($26,520)		($53,040)
Telephone & Communications		($7,600)		($6,700)		($3,484)		($6,968)
Legal & Professional		($10,000)		($10,200)		($5,304)		($10,608)
Management Fee		($72,400)		($75,000)		($39,000)		($78,000)
Marketing		($10,000)		($9,700)		($5,044)		($10,088)
Office & Administrative		($20,000)		($20,800)		($10,816)		($21,632)
Miscellaneous		($5,000)		($4,000)		($2,080)		($4,160)
Replacement Reserves		($20,000)		($37,000)		($10,000)		($20,000)
TOTAL OPERATING EXPENSES		($400,000)		($428,300)		($212,700)		($425,400)
NET OPERATING INCOME (NOI)*		$1,291,200		$1,422,200		$750,000		$1,500,000

* Net cash flow before debt service

flow." Financial terms such as these are not uniform among lenders and may have different connotations. So it's important not to get hung up on the title. However, it's important to note the use of the words "underwriting" and "stabilized." The word "underwriting" in this context is an adjective and therefore suggests that this type of cash flow is unique and exclusive of all other cash flows. This particular cash flow estimate is the one used by the bank's underwriter, hence the expression "underwriting cash flow." This term refers to a relatively safe and conservative cash flow estimate used in establishing the size of the loan. The loan analysis page is a mock underwriting exercise that attempts to demonstrate to the lender that there is sufficient cash flow to support the requested loan. The word "stabilized" refers to a consistent and predictable series of cash flows that has been tested over time, which is the reason the loan analysis includes two to three years of historical income and expenses.

Certain underwriting assumptions must be applied in order to establish the underwriting cash flow and may result in a lower "underwritten" net operating income (NOI). For example, as illustrated in Figure 2-7 the underwriting assumptions and expense adjustments used in calculating the underwriting cash flow resulted in an "underwritten" NOI that is lower than the actual NOI for years 2007, 2008, and 2009 annualized. There is also a place to input the number of units, net rentable square feet, the capitalization rate, purchase price and loan amount, interest rate, and length of amortization, which will all be used to calculate the annual debt service. Once the historical, annualized, and underwriting columns are completed, the model will automatically calculate the debt coverage ratio (DCR), the loan-to-value ratio (LTV), and market value. The example shown in Figure 2-7 represents a typical single page underwriting cash flow model for a 240-unit multifamily complex complete with DCR and LTV ratios and an estimated market value calculated at the bottom of the spreadsheet. Each unique loan analysis must be customized

Figure 2-7. Loan Analysis.

Underwriting Cash Flow Model			
Purchase Price	$10,000,000	Interest Rate	7.00%
Loan Amount	$8,000,000	Amortization (years)	30
Loan-to-Cost (LTC)	80.0%	Annual Debt Service	($638,690)
Property Type:	Multi-family		
Total Units	240		
Total Rentable SF	260,000		

	Jan.-Dec 2007	Jan.-Dec 2008	Year-to-Date Annualized 2009	Underwriting Cash Flow
GROSS POTENTIAL INCOME	$2,505,600	$2,600,000	$2,600,000	$2,600,000
Loss to Lease	($150,000)	($100,000)	($70,000)	($100,000)
Gross Rental Income (actual)	$2,355,600	$2,500,000	$2,530,000	$2,500,000
Vacancy & Collection Loss	($350,000)	($265,000)	($180,000)	($250,000)
NET RENTAL INCOME	$2,005,600	$2,235,000	$2,350,000	$2,250,000
OTHER INCOME				
Late Fees	$16,873	$15,000	$10,400	$10,400
Laundry & Vending	$2,052	$2,000	$7,400	$7,400
Application Fees	$7,949	$5,000	$5,800	$5,800
TOTAL	$26,874	$22,000	$23,600	$23,600
EFFECTIVE GROSS INCOME (EGI)	$2,032,474	$2,257,000	$2,373,600	$2,273,600
EXPENSES				
Real Estate Taxes	($250,000)	($275,000)	($290,000)	($290,000)
Insurance	($85,000)	($90,000)	($92,000)	($94,760)
Utilities	($208,374)	($211,000)	($208,000)	($214,240)
Trash	($32,341)	($33,000)	($29,200)	($30,076)
Pest Control	($487)	($5,000)	($5,600)	($5,768)
Telephone & Communications	($3,305)	($3,400)	($3,900)	($4,017)
Repairs & Maintenance	($83,054)	($124,000)	($153,000)	($146,664)
Cleaning & Make Ready	($16,595)	($20,000)	($50,000)	($51,500)
Salaries & Payroll Taxes	($274,577)	($302,000)	($300,000)	($309,000)
Security	($5,000)	($4,800)	($6,400)	($12,750)
Management Fee	($55,000)	($67,710)	($94,880)	($90,944)
Nonrevenue Units	($8,600)	($12,000)	($14,500)	($14,935)
Legal & Professional	($6,175)	($5,000)	($9,400)	($15,000)
Advertising & Marketing	($15,000)	($18,000)	($11,200)	($20,000)
General & Administrative	($12,152)	($13,000)	($35,520)	($36,586)
Miscellaneous	($14,424)	($10,000)	($10,000)	($12,000)
Replacement Reserves	($85,000)	($125,000)	($60,000)	($72,000)
TOTAL OPERATING EXPENSES	($1,155,084)	($1,318,910)	($1,373,600)	($1,420,240)
NET OPERATING INCOME (NOI)*	$877,390	$938,090	$1,000,000	$853,360

Net cash flow before debt service

(continues)

Figure 2-7. (Continued.)

DCR ANALYSIS					
Annual Debt Service (1st Lien)		($638,690)	($638,690)	($638,690)	($638,690)
Debt Coverage Ratio (DCR)		1.37	1.47	1.57	1.34
Annual Debt Service (2nd Lien)		($215,000)	($215,000)	($215,000)	($215,000)
Combined DCR		1.03	1.10	1.17	1.00
LOAN TO VALUE ANALYSIS (LTV)					
Capitalized NOI @	8.0%	$10,967,375	$11,726,125	$12,500,000	$10,667,005
Value per Unit		$45,697	$48,859	$52,083	$44,446
Value per SF		$42.18	$45.10	$48.08	$41.03
Loan-to-Value (LTC)		72.94%	68.22%	64.00%	75.00%

depending on the property type, structure of the loan, and level of details within the financial statements. The complexity of the loan analysis also depends on whether the request is for a construction, bridge, or fixed-rate term loan.

Supporting Documents

The fourth and last part of the property economics section of the loan request package should include a complete set of *supporting documents* used in preparing the schedule of income, historical cash flow summary, and loan analysis. These supporting documents are necessary for verification and cross-reference. Lenders usually do not have any reason to question the borrower's or broker's analysis and assume that the pro forma cash flow or underwriting cash flow used to size the loan is accurate and substantiated. However, many loan officers or analysts prefer to conduct their own preliminary underwriting and analysis using the actual rent roll and operating statements. Therefore, be sure to include in the property economics section, if at all possible, the following list of supporting documents:

➤ Rent roll
➤ Property income and expense statements
➤ A trailing twelve-month income and expense statement (if available)

- ➤ Occupancy history
- ➤ Lease rollover schedule (if available)
- ➤ Construction budget (for brand new ground-up construction loans)
- ➤ Renovation budget
- ➤ Capital repair budget

Market and Submarket Data

The *market* and *submarket data* section of the loan request package provides the lender with vital market and submarket statistics such as average rental rates, rental concessions, rental rate trends, operating expense ratios, vacancy and occupancy rates, absorption rates, inventory ratios, average sale prices, and new construction activity. This section primarily highlights supply and demand data based on property type within the subject property's market and submarket. The word "market" refers to a general region such as a city or metropolis (metro area). The word "submarket," on the other hand, refers to a much smaller region within the overall market. There are numerous submarkets found within a general market or metro area. The submarket is of particular interest to a lender because that's where competition directly impacts the subject property. Just for clarification, the phrase "subject property" refers to the property that needs to be financed. You may be asking yourself at this point: Why do I need to provide all of this market and submarket information and, after all, isn't that the job of a professional commercial real estate appraiser? Yes, it is the job of a commercial appraiser, but often appraisals are not ordered until after the issue of a letter of interest by the lender. In order to get that letter of interest, a lender needs to feel comfortable about the health and strength of the subject property's submarket. Specifically, a lender needs proof that monthly rental rates, concessions, vacancy rates, operating expenses, and cap rates used in estimating the net operating income and market value of the subject property are comparable to those of competing properties and, moreover, are sustainable. Many times pro forma estimates are overstated without any justification, as if someone had pulled the numbers right out of the air. The purpose of this section is to reassure the lender that income and expense and market value estimates used by the borrower, mortgage broker, or broker's analyst are well within the range of averages found in the property's submarket. Be sure to customize the market study to fit the characteristics and likeness of the subject property. Otherwise, the lender may draw conclusions from her own market study and ultimately reject your loan request.

Market and submarket data can be gleaned from various market surveys and submarket reports prepared by regional and national market research and commercial real estate firms such as Co-Star, REIS, Cushman & Wakefield, CB Richard Ellis, and Grubb & Ellis. All of these firms provide commercial real estate research and analysis on a quarterly basis for all property types, including multifamily, office, retail, and industrial (office-warehouse), which they often publish free as a tool for marketing their brokerage services. However, not all commercial real estate market research firms, such as Co-Star and REIS, offer free surveys. You don't necessarily need to include a general market study or survey in this section because most local lenders are already familiar with the local market. An out-of-state lender, on the other hand, who is not familiar with a local market might benefit from a general market survey, so try to include one, if at all possible.

As previously mentioned, the health and strength of a submarket, generally speaking, are more important to the lender than the condition of the overall market. For whatever reason, some submarkets are insulated from the declining rents and falling property values that are plaguing other parts of the city. In this situation, it might not be a good idea to include a metro market study for fear of spooking the lender. A submarket survey can be a detailed professional report full of graphs, charts, and tables prepared by one of the aforementioned commercial real estate firms, or it can be as simple as a one- or two-page list of comparable rental properties that compete directly with the subject property. The purpose here is to disclose and reveal the fundamentals of the submarket area, such as the sub-market's overall occupancy and vacancy rates, average rental rates, rental rate trends (percentage increases/decreases), new construction activity, and absorption rates. It is also a good idea to include a list of comparable sales, preferably within the past year, that support the estimated market value presented in the property economics section. Following is a list of information that is basic to any comparable rental and comparable sales survey.

Rent Comparables

- Name of property
- Photo
- Address
- Distance from subject property
- Size (square feet, number of units)
- Year built
- Occupancy
- Rental rates
- Type of lease (e.g., NNN, full service)
- Number of tenants
- Rent specials or concessions, if any
- Operating expenses
- Base year or expense stop

Sales Comparables

- Name of property
- Photo
- Address
- Distance from subject property
- Size (square feet, number of units)
- Year built
- Occupancy
- Total sales price
- Sales price per unit or per SF
- Date of sale

Sponsorship

The *Sponsorship* section of the loan request package is where the lender can find information about the financial strength and experience of the sponsorship. The word "sponsorship" is really industry jargon for borrowers, key principals, and guarantors. The origin of this word is not known, but it refers to the person or persons who will be ultimately responsible for the care and operation of the property and for the repayment of the loan.

This section should begin with an overview of the borrower's commercial real estate background and experience. A company or personal business resumé will suffice, but be sure it includes information such as years of commercial real estate experience, the number, size, and type of projects owned, constructed, or renovated over the years, and a list of achievements, professional affiliations and trade organizations, professional licenses, and unique skills. A list of business partners or affiliates is also helpful to someone trying to understand the extent of the borrower's knowledge and scope of work. The borrower's experience is just as important as the borrower's balance sheet. A strong balance sheet alone, such as one showing a high net worth, will get the borrower nowhere with a lender real fast if the borrower has no experience whatsoever. Throwing money at a problem is not what a lender likes to see, so keep in mind that a resumé with remarkable and striking credentials can every now and then trump a weak balance sheet.

In addition to a company or business resumé, the sponsorship section must include a set of personal financial statements. A set of personal financial statements consists of three standard accounting documents: a balance sheet, an income statement, and a cash flow statement. The balance sheet helps the lender determine the borrower's liquidity and net worth and is the most important document of the three. The income statement discloses the borrower's total earnings or annual income. The cash flow statement is extremely helpful in pinning down the borrower's personal cash flow, which is different from the income statement. These financial documents are usually prepared by the borrower's accountant. If the borrower is a small, unsophisticated investor or does not employ an accountant to create such documents, she can either use a preprinted bank form or create a set of financial statements from scratch. There are numerous sources available for producing these financial documents. Most banks have preprinted forms that a borrower can use. A real estate schedule referred to as the REO Schedule is also needed. This is not a typical financial or accounting document but a list of real estate assets owned by the borrower. Net worth, liquidity, personal cash flow, and the REO Schedule are discussed in Chapters 3 and 5. Following is a list of resumés, financial statements, and personal documents commonly found in the Sponsorship section:

- ➤ Borrower's personal resumé
- ➤ Borrower's company resumé
- ➤ Balance sheet
- ➤ Income statement
- ➤ Cash flow statement
- ➤ REO schedule
- ➤ Copy of credit report

FINANCIAL STRENGTH AND CREDITWORTHINESS

Commercial real estate lenders base their decision to fund commercial real estate loans on two primary conditions; the strength and consistency of the property's cash flow and on the financial strength and creditworthiness of the borrower. As previously discussed in Chapter 1, analyzing the strength and consistency of the property's cash flow is referred to as property underwriting, and analyzing the financial strength and creditworthiness of the borrower involves underwriting the borrower. The process of underwriting the borrower is the topic of Chapter 3, which includes a detailed discussion of financial strength and creditworthiness and examines personal *net worth*, *liquidity*, and *free cash flow*.

Net Worth and Liquidity

Net worth on paper may look fairly impressive at first glance, but, from the perspective of a commercial real estate lender, this opinion of one's worth is nothing more than wishful thinking on the part of the borrower. Net worth is relative, and one should always be reminded that net worth on paper is entirely different from the borrower's true or actual net worth. Often we hear someone bragging about someone else's net worth, but what is net worth and what does it really mean? Personal net worth is the equity or residual interest in the assets of a person or an entity that remains after deducting liabilities. In other words, it is simply the difference between the total value of all assets less the total of all liabilities. Net worth, also referred to as *owner's equity,* is found on the borrower's balance sheet. Accounting firms and accountants typically use the term "owner's equity" in lieu of "net worth," though both really mean the same thing. In the definition of net worth the words "equity" or "residual interest" in the value of an asset refer to *capital.* Whether the borrower's capital is in the form of cash only or in cash and appreciation is a question only a balance sheet can help answer. Analyzing a borrower's net worth always begins with a review of a borrower's balance sheet. Balance sheets are a part of a set of personal financial statements usually prepared by the borrower or the borrower's accountant. An *audited financial statement,* or, specifically, the balance sheet, prepared and audited by an accountant or a certified public accountant (CPA), is usually preferred by lenders to a balance sheet prepared by the borrower. A set of *compiled financial statements* prepared by a CPA, though not yet audited, is also acceptable by lenders. A balance sheet prepared by an accountant or a CPA is much more reliable than one prepared personally by the borrower because borrowers tend to invariably overstate the value of their assets. That's not to say that an accountant can't get it wrong, too, since much of the financial information comes directly from the borrower. There are many other errors made by borrowers that either overstate their assets or understate their liabilities, but the single most common error on nearly every balance sheet that is not prepared by a CPA is inflated values. A lender will question these values and in most cases adjust the total value of all the assets down to a lower, more realistic figure. Liabilities and debts, on the other hand, are usually not overstated but are often understated or intentionally omitted, resulting in an exaggerated net worth.

Assets

Let's examine the asset side of the balance sheet, which is where most of the errors and value exaggerations occur. Lenders often find inconsistencies and ambiguous values that seem to have been pulled right out of the air. There are many types of *short-term* and *long-term assets*, both *tangible* and *intangible*. Short-term assets, also referred to as *current assets*, generally include cash, marketable securities, receivables, inventories, prepaid expenses, and other assets, which are expected to be converted into cash, sold, or used in the operations of the business, usually within a year. *Long-term assets*, also referred to as *fixed assets*, generally include real property and plant and equipment used in the operations of the business, which will be held for many years. Tangible assets are assets that have physical substance, such as land, buildings, real property, automobiles, manufacturing equipment, and inventory. Intangible assets have value, like tangible assets, but do not have physical substance; they include franchises, patents, copyrights, trademarks, and goodwill. Aside from pointing out the difference between short-term and long-term assets and tangible and intangible assets, we should mention one more distinction, and that is the distinction between *non–real estate assets* and *real estate assets*. Non–real estate assets and real estate assets are not subcategories found on a balance sheet but are internal asset classes used by commercial real estate lenders. The distinction between the two asset classes helps the lender identify the primary source of a borrower's net worth, which is discussed later in this chapter.

Commercial real estate lenders are not like commercial bankers. They don't lend to businesses that are engaged in manufacturing, production, or retail services that generate revenue from producing or rendering goods and services. These types of businesses generally involve the ownership, use, and manufacture of different types of non–real estate assets (excluding plant and equipment), both tangible and intangible and are integral to the operations and profitability of the business. Non–real estate assets of an enterprise such as these are of little value to a commercial real estate lender, since, after all, the primary interest of a commercial real estate lender is to lend money for the purchase or refinance of an income-producing property that produces cash flow, not for the purchase of special-use facilities that are owner-occupied. This distinction is important because commercial real estate lenders understand real estate and real estate only. Non–real estate assets, with the exception of cash, CDs, stock, bonds, and marketable securities, used for or related to other types of businesses are rarely used as collateral and often are excluded in calculating a borrower's net worth. The issue of non–real estate assets versus real estate assets in relation to net worth is especially relevant when or if the value of the property securing the loan unexpectedly falls below the loan amount. And if the borrower defaults on the loan, resulting in a huge loss for the lender, how will the lender recover the loss? This is where the true test of a borrower's financial strength comes into play, and that depends squarely on whether a borrower's net worth consists primarily of real estate assets or non–real estate assets. Borrowers who have sufficient real estate assets and who own other commercial properties are much stronger than those that don't and are less likely to default on the loan. The presumption here is that there is ample equity in the real estate assets (separate and apart from non–real estate assets), which can be converted into enough cash to pay in full the loan that is in default or at least cover the deficiency if the lender is forced to sell the property for less than the original loan amount. Conversely, borrowers who have only non–real estate assets that cannot be converted to cash relatively quickly and that are integral to the operation of other businesses are more likely to default on the loan. Lenders doubt that these non–real estate assets can be sold at their full stated value or sold at all.

Non–Real Estate Assets

Non–real estate assets include both short-term and long-term assets excluding real property, with the exception of land, plant, and equipment of an owner-occupied facility used in manufacturing and distribution (in the context of this discussion regarding non–real estate assets, land, plant, and equipment are treated more as fixed capital than real property). Examples of non–real estate assets include just about any type of asset not classified as real property, such as cash, stocks, bonds, marketable securities, account receivables, note receivables, goodwill, inventory, prepaid expenses, tools, jewelry, retirement accounts, automobiles, and equity in net assets of a partnership or subsidiary. The problem with most non–real estate assets such as stock in a private corporation, trusts, equity in net assets of a partnership or subsidiary, time shares, account receivables, or even patents and trademarks is that their monetary worths are just mere guesses, with no justification given for their assumed values. There is no way for a commercial real estate lender to verify the veracity of these stated values, and that's why a balance sheet prepared by a CPA is preferred to one prepared by the borrower. A lender is much more likely to believe in the monetary values of non–real estate assets if they have been prepared by a CPA, since, after all, these values are reported to the IRS. All of these non–real estate assets may be assets, technically speaking, but to a commercial real estate lender they are of little value as collateral for a commercial real estate loan. In reality, a lender has no use for these non–real estate assets because they are difficult to liquidate and fall outside the expertise and understanding of a commercial real estate lender. A commercial real estate lender understands real estate only and thus really and truly likes to see real estate assets above all other asset classes on a borrower's balance sheet.

As previously mentioned, lenders often exclude several non–real estate assets from the calculation of net worth. The main reason that they are often disregarded is that non–real estate assets are difficult to liquidate and at best extremely difficult to value. In a commercial real estate lender's mind, these assets can be difficult to sell; even if they can be sold, the lender will question how much cash will be raised by the borrower in the event that the borrower needs to liquidate his assets to meet the obligation on a loan that was secured by a property that failed to retain its value. So, then, which non–real estate assets are worthy, and which ones are not? Following is a list of non–real estate assets, which are separated into those assets excluded and those that are included in the calculation of a borrower's net worth:

Assets that are *excluded*:
- Trusts
- Noncontrolling ownership interests
- Stocks in private corporations
- Unsecured notes receivable
- Life insurance policies
- Business equipment and inventory
- Personal loans
- Equity in net assets of a partnership

Assets that are *included*:
- Cash (checking, savings, and money market accounts)
- Certificates of Deposit (CDs)
- Stocks
- Bonds
- Mutual funds
- Notes receivable supported by real estate
- Lender escrow reserve accounts

- Company stock options
- Automobiles, personal property, jewelry, guns
- Oil and gas interests
- Accounts receivable
- Time shares
- Nonpublicly traded securities
- Goodwill, patents, trademarks

- IRAs, 401(k)s, pension
- Earnest money escrowed at title company
- Precious metal bullion

Real Estate Assets, Cash Equity, and Market Equity

Owner's equity, also referred to as net worth, is the residual owner-ship interest in the value of any asset after deducting its liabilities. This definition of owner's equity also applies to *real estate assets.* For example, if a property is worth $5 million and there is a mortgage of $3 million, the owner is presumed to have an owner's equity or resid-ual ownership interest in the value of the property equal to $2 mil-lion. Now if this property is the borrower's only asset and assuming there are no other non–real estate assets, such as cash, stocks, or marketable securities, the borrower's net worth is the same as his owner's equity of $2 million. In this situation, net worth and owner's equity are one and the same. From this point forward, the discussion concerning owner's equity and net worth is based on the assumption that total net worth is no different from owner's total equity in each and every real estate asset.

Total owner's equity or net worth is usually composed of both *cash equity* and *market equity.* Depending on the ratio or balance of cash equity to market equity, the lender's net worth requirement will vary. Let's say a borrower's net worth is $5 million, of which $1 mil-lion is in cash and $4 million is market equity. Market equity is the difference between the current debt and the appraised value of the property regardless of the original cost. For example, if an investor

paid $3 million for the purchase of an apartment complex and bor-
rowed $2 million, his initial cash equity would be $1 million. But
suppose that, years later, the property appraises for $4 million and
the investor still owes $2 million; the investor's market equity is now
$2 million, even though the investor had an original cash equity of
only $1 million. In this illustration, the investor's market equity of $2
million is in reality a combination of $1 million in cash and $1 million in appreciation. Usually, after a year, lenders will allow the use
of market equity in lieu of cash equity if they agree with the market
values shown on the borrower's balance sheet.

Now let's say that the borrower wants to borrow $5 million for the
purchase of a retail shopping center. In this situation, the borrower's
net worth of $5 million is equal to the amount the investor wants to
borrow, which means that it is sufficient to pay back the entire $5
million loan. However, lenders know that, no matter what happens,
the risk of losing the entire $5 million loan is unlikely because the
property will always retain some amount of value even if it is 100 percent vacant. Properties will always have residual land value along
with some salvageable value because of the improvements (building
fixtures, parking garage). Even if the lender has to foreclose on the
property and later sells it for 30 percent of its original value, the
lender will never face a 100 percent loss. So, in reality, the lender's
potential loss is never 100 percent of the $5 million loan. A borrow-
er's net worth, therefore, does not need to be equal to the loan
amount. For example, suppose the investor pays $6.250 million and
borrows 80 percent, or $5 million. Two years later, the retail center is
hit hard by the downturn in the local economy due to the loss of a
major employer. The tenants cannot survive this downturn, and
eventually break their leases and vacate the retail center, leaving the
investor no cash flow to pay back the loan. The investor defaults on
the loan and the lender forecloses, taking back the property. One year
later, the lender finally sells the property for $3 million, or approxi-

mately $0.48 on the dollar (the original purchase price was $6.250 million). However, the original loan balance was only $5 million. The lender therefore records a loss of $2 million (most likely this was a full recourse loan, making the borrower liable for the lender's loss of $2 million).

As mentioned earlier, the borrower's total net worth was $5 million, which is more than sufficient to cover the lender's loss. Remember that the borrower had $1 million in cash and $4 million in market equity. In this situation, the borrower is liable for the lender's loss and has to pay the lender $2 million in cash. Since the borrower has only $1 million in cash, the rest has to come from the sale of one or more of the borrower's properties to raise another $1 million in cash to cover the $2 million loss to the lender. In this example, the borrower's minimum net worth would have had to have been at least $2 million (or 40%) of the $5 million loan to adequately cover the lender's $2 million loss. But this is really cutting it close. The lender would have taken a big risk if they had approved the $5 million loan based on a $2 million net worth. If the borrower's minimum net worth of $2 million were in all cash, that would have been acceptable to the lender, but if it was $500,000 in cash and the rest in long-term assets, it is unlikely that the borrower would have been approved for a $5 million loan on the basis of that mix of cash equity and market equity.

Lenders do not use a standard formula to calculate the minimum net worth of a borrower, but a general rule of thumb is that net worth should generally be equal to the loan amount. The minimum net worth a borrower must have is about 50 percent of the requested loan amount. In the foregoing illustration, the general rule of thumb would have required that the borrower's net worth be at least 50 percent, or $2.5 million of the $5 million loan request. But before the borrower's net worth can be considered sufficient, whether it is 50 percent, 60 percent, or even double the loan amount, it is important to first examine the borrower's balance sheet and question those assets that are often disregarded by most real estate lenders. The review and examination of the balance sheet should result in an adjusted net worth that excludes non–real estate assets, both intangible and tangible, as previously demonstrated in the Non–Real Estate Assets section. It is not uncommon for a real estate lender to lower a borrower's net worth by 50 percent or even more. This is the single most exaggerated part of a borrower's financial statement. The statements are not necessarily fraudulent, but exaggerations do put into question the borrower's truthfulness. An inaccurate representation of the borrower's financial well-being does not bode well when the lender is making a financial credit decision.

Cost vs. Market Value

Another concern for lenders is the issue of *cost* versus *market value* as it relates to real estate assets. Are the values listed on the asset side of the balance sheet stated at their original cost, or are they stated at market or appraised value (this discussion does not include non–real estate assets, since their values, whether cost or market, are usually not factored in when lenders are estimating a borrower's net worth)? Which does the lender prefer? That depends on whether the asset is a recently acquired asset or one that has been owned for several years. The general rule is that if a real estate asset has been owned for less than one year, it is best to state the value at cost plus any capital improvements to truly reflect the borrower's cash cost. Often a borrower will have had the property reappraised within the first year of ownership, which may or may not result in a value significantly higher than the original purchase price. If the appraised value came in significantly higher, then the borrower will most likely boast of this new value and will want to show his newfound net worth on his balance sheet. However, lenders prefer that these properties be seasoned for at least a year before they will start using the appraised values in determining a borrower's net worth. The problem with appraised values, especially those estimated within less than one year of ownership, is that the value estimate is based on pro forma figures, which may have not yet been realized. In other words, the actual cash flow has not yet stabilized, and if the property has to be sold, especially under pressure because of a borrower's inability to pay off an unrelated loan, it is likely to bring in a price far below the appraised value.

Even if the borrower has owned the properties for years and is using current market values, the lender may still question whether they are really worth the values estimated by the borrower. How were these values estimated? Does the borrower have recent appraisal reports to support these values, or did the borrower capitalize the NOI at some market capitalization rate to derive their values? Borrowers tend to overstate property values, bringing into question the borrower's overall net worth, which is why these values must be verified. If the property values cannot be verified, the lender will just start hacking away at the values using their own best estimates, resulting in a final value estimate that will no doubt lower the borrower's net worth. When in doubt, it is always best to instruct the borrower to list real estate assets at their original cost if at all possible; if the market values listed are justified, be prepared to defend them by providing either the property's most recent P&L statement or a copy of the most recent appraisal report (preferably dated within the past year), along with the balance sheet.

Pre-Funding Liquidity

Pre-funding liquidity simply refers to the borrower's level of liquidity prior to funding the loan. Use of the term is essentially a definitive way to distinguish the borrower's overall level of liquidity from the borrower's post-funding liquidity and nothing more. *Liquidity* is the single most important quality of a creditworthy borrower. Liquidity refers to the borrower's ability to convert readily available short-term assets into cash or U.S. currency in a timely manner, usually within a few days. Unlike long-term assets, which can take months or years to sell, liquid assets can be converted to cash within days and are the most sought-after assets on a balance sheet. Liquid assets include both cash and noncash assets and therefore are included in the calculation of net worth. Even though net worth is important, commercial real estate lenders also want to know how much of that net worth is liquid. Liquidity is a measure of the borrower's ability to withstand financial hardship. The portion or percentage of cash and short-term assets that can be converted into cash within a few days is commonly referred to as a *liquidity ratio*. Standard liquidity ratios usually equal 10 percent or 20 percent of the borrower's net worth. Examples of liquid assets include the following:

Cash assets
Checking and savings accounts
Money market accounts
Certificates of deposits (CDs)
Earnest money held in escrow
Trust accounts (only if the trust is a guarantor and if it is a family trust; restricted and charitable trusts cannot guarantee debt)
Capital replacement reserves

Marketable securities (noncash assets)
Stocks
Bonds
Mutual funds

Short-term assets that are often mistaken for liquid assets include individual retirement accounts (IRAs); employer retirement accounts, such as 401(k)s; pensions; and other vested retirement funds. Retirement accounts are disqualified as liquid assets for two reasons. The first problem is that there are significant early-withdrawal penalties and income taxes if funds are withdrawn prematurely, which effectively deters a borrower from using the cash. The second is that IRA accounts and 401(k)s are usually protected from liquidation or seizure in a personal bankruptcy, rendering them inaccessible to any creditor. Also, if a borrower is essentially retired and is drawing on these retirement funds, lenders consider them as sources of income only and not as sources of cash to repay any debt. If the borrower has significant income from a salaried job or from real estate investments, only then will the lender consider the IRAs as a liquid asset, but this is not often the case. In summary, pre-funding liquidity should equal approximately 10 percent of a borrower's total net worth. Keep in mind that this percentage ratio is just a general rule of thumb. Some lenders may want to see that figure as high as 20 percent.

Post-Funding Liquidity

In a refinance, depending on whether the loan involves cash out to the borrower, *post-funding liquidity* does not differ from *pre-funding liquidity*. However, if the loan is for the acquisition of a property and is not a refinance, post-funding liquidity will decrease by an amount equal to the dollar amount of the down payment. *Post-funding liquidity* is the amount of cash the borrower has remaining after the loan has been funded. Whether the loan is for a refinance or a purchase, there are usually financing and closing costs, fees, and down payments involved that result in a "Cash (from) Borrower" figure on the purchaser's side of the settlement statement. This "Cash (from) Borrower" figure is the actual amount of cash a borrower must bring to the closing. So it is essential that the estimated settlement charges and the down payment be excluded from the calculation of a borrower's post-funding liquidity. In the lender's eyes, it is not enough just to prove liquidity for the purpose of consummating the transaction; it is a litmus test that demonstrates financial wherewithal and staying power. For example, if it takes every penny the borrower has to fund the loan, leaving the borrower with no cash whatsoever, and then all of a sudden there is an unexpected major breakdown or necessary repair at the property or, even worse, damage from hail or wind, where will the borrower get the money to remedy the problem? If there is storm damage, how will the borrower pay the required $5,000 or $10,000 deductible? If the borrower cannot meet the deductible, the insurance company may not pay the claim. Without sufficient cash reserves, the borrower will be unable to make repairs or pay the insurance deductible, which in turn may result in loss of occupancy and cash flow. And what about a sudden loss of occupancy that reduces the income so significantly that there isn't enough cash flow to make the monthly mortgage payment? For this reason, lenders require post-funding liquidity of some predetermined amount. But how much is enough?

In general, post-funding liquidity should equal at least six months' worth of monthly debt service, if not more. Some lenders actually require twelve months' worth of debt service; it depends on the lender's credit policy, which does change from time to time to reflect current economic conditions. Monthly debt service is another way of referring to the monthly principal and interest (P&I) payments. For example, six months' worth of monthly principal and interest payments of $10,000 will require at least $60,000 in post-funding liquidity ($10,000 × 6 months = $60,000). Post-funding liquidity less than $60,000, in this example, is inadequate and may result in the denial of the loan.

The minimum level of post-funding liquidity can also be calculated by multiplying the loan amount by 10 percent. For example, a loan of $2 million will require at least $200,000 in post-funding liquidity, preferably in cash ($2,000,000 × .10 = $200,000). However, for a loan of this size, 10 percent may be too high. In fact, the 10 percent rule results in a significantly higher post-funding liquidity requirement of $200,000 than does the six-month rule, which results in a requirement of $60,000. If the difference between the two methods is significant, as in this example, a lender may split the difference or just use the lower value of the two. This is a judgment call by the underwriter and depends on other underwriting factors, such as strength in the property cash flow and loan to value. However, if a borrower can demonstrate this kind of financial strength, there is a 90 percent chance that a lender will look favorably on the loan request and drop the 10 percent rule.

Lender's Calculation of Net Worth and Pre-Funding and Post-Funding Liquidity

Commercial real estate lenders are skeptical by nature and often project a negative outlook, which explains why they are extremely conservative. They routinely assume the worst-case scenario in all transactions and factor in contingencies. It is for this reason that lenders often challenge asset values enumerated on a balance sheet. If asset values declared by the borrower are suspect, then liquidity and net worth may be suspect, as well. Borrowers, whether intentionally or not, tend to overstate asset values or simply misrepresent their net worth. Lenders, on the other hand, embrace their own opinion of value regarding liquidity and net worth and as a consequence take the liberty of calculating a completely different set of values. Lenders modify liquidity and net worth by either reducing the assets' underlying value or excluding them from the balance sheet altogether. Figure 3-1 is an example of an unaudited balance sheet prepared by the borrower, absent any supporting financial schedules and notes. Without supporting documentation, such as real estate schedules, financial notes, and tax returns, real estate lenders are often left in the dark and are forced to make undocumented assumptions regarding not only the origin of these asset values but their reliability, as well. If there were a way to independently verify the accuracy of these asset values, lenders would certainly take that approach, but often that is neither practical nor possible. It is this skepticism that compels lenders to closely examine each line-item asset and to determine whether or not to exclude a particular asset from their own estimate of liquidity and net worth. This underwriting exercise or, more specifically, modification by the lender is not an attempt to undermine the borrower's ego but is simply a stress test intended to accurately reflect the borrower's true liquidity and net worth. The following discussion demonstrates how lenders calculate *net worth* and *prefunding* and *post-funding liquidity*.

The sample balance sheet illustrated in Figure 3-1 includes two columns, one with an unadjusted net worth and one with an adjusted or revised net worth. The second column, labeled "Lender's Adjustment," is nothing more than a duplication of the first column and does not represent a standard balance sheet. As illustrated in the first column, the borrower's unadjusted net worth is $8 million. However, the second column indicates an adjusted or revised net worth equal to $4,301,500. The adjusted net worth is the result of the lender's scrutiny of individual line-item assets. When the relevancy or value of these assets are in doubt and the borrower cannot provide a satisfactory answer or supporting documentation, the assets are simply excluded from the calculation of the borrower's net worth.

As demonstrated in Figure 3-1, the lender begins by crossing out two short-term assets, *accounts receivable* and a *life insurance policy*. Receivables in general are assets representing the claims that a bor-

Figure 3-1. Lender Adjusted Balance Sheet.

BALANCE SHEET		
ASSETS		Lender's Adjustment
Current (Short-Term) Assets:		
Checking & Savings		
Earnest Money Deposit *	$50,000	$50,000
Checking Accounts *	$150,000	$150,000
Savings Account *	$750,000	$750,000
Certificate of Deposits *	$450,000	$450,000
Marketable Securities		
Stocks *	$580,000	$580,000
Bonds *	$72,000	$72,000
Mutual Funds *	$675,000	$675,000
Nonmarketable Securities	$0	$0
Accounts Receivable	$35,000	$~~35,000~~
Cash Value of Life Insurance Policy	$100,000	$~~100,000~~
Fixed (Long-Term) Assets:		
Notes Receivable	$2,350,000	$~~2,350,000~~
Real Estate (Homestead)	$500,000	$500,000
Real Estate (Investments)	$6,000,000	$6,000,000
Vested interest in IRAs & Pension & Retirement Plans	$275,000	$275,000
Investment in Partnerships	$750,000	$~~750,000~~
Business Equipment & Inventory		
Oil & Gas Interests	$35,000	$~~35,000~~
Trusts		
Company Stock Options (Exercisable)	$42,000	$42,000
Time Shares	$7,500	$~~7,500~~
Goodwill	$100,000	$~~100,000~~
Other Assets		
Personal Property	$150,000	$~~150,000~~
Automobiles, Boats	$76,000	$~~76,000~~
Art, Jewelry	$35,000	$~~35,000~~
Gun Collection	$15,000	$~~15,000~~
Furniture	$45,000	$~~45,000~~
TOTAL ASSETS	$13,242,500	$9,544,000

(continues)

Figure 3-1. (Continued)

LIABILITIES

Notes Payable	$473,000	$473,000
Real Estate Mortgages (Homestead)	$300,000	$300,000
Real Estate Mortgages (Investments)	$4,250,000	$4,250,000
Security Deposits	$26,000	$26,000
Payroll Taxes	$23,000	$23,000
Federal & State Income Tax	$60,000	$60,000
Installment Loans	$7,500	$7,500
Credit Cards	$63,000	$63,000
Automobile Loans	$40,000	$40,000
TOTAL LIABILITIES	$5,242,500	$5,242,500
NET WORTH	**$8,000,000**	**$4,301,500**
TOTAL LIABILITIES & NET WORTH	$13,242,500	$9,544,000

rower has against others. In particular, accounts receivable are extensions of credit to customers for either the purchase of merchandise or the rendering of services. Accounts receivable are not supported by "formal" or written promises to pay and are totally at risk. In other words, an account receivable represents the dollar amount a borrower claims that he or she is owed by a third party, whether an individual or company. Though these types of assets are transferable, commercial real estate lenders often consider them worthless. The problem is that a certain percentage of the receivables are never collected. Also, receivables are not secured. Instead of trying to guess at the probability of repayment, a lender will just dismiss this asset altogether. The cash value of a life insurance policy is usually a negligible amount of money, and policies are rarely cashed in by borrowers, even in bankruptcy.

Moving down the balance sheet, the lender identifies five more questionable long-term (fixed) assets and begins by eliminating *notes receivable*. Notes receivable are long-term loans or claims against others, usually supported by "formal" or written promises to pay. These may or may not be negotiable instruments depending on such factors as the terms, form, and content of the note. An example of a note receivable would be a seller note or personal loan to a third party. It is also important to note that these types of loans or claims may not be secured, putting repayment of the loan at risk. In the case of a seller note, often referred to as seller financing, the borrower may have secured his personal loan by placing a lien against the land or building. Though the lien may protect the borrower from loss, it does not necessarily guarantee payment of the debt. Whether or not note receivables are secured, repayment is not guaranteed and can take years. It is for this reason that lenders often exclude notes receivable from the calculation of net worth.

Investments in partnerships, businesses, or *other non–real estate ventures* are very difficult to liquidate. They are also very difficult to value by a lender. A borrower may say that he invested $750,000 in cash and list it as an asset, but the money is most likely already capitalized, so the borrower has no way of withdrawing the original cash investment until the company authorizes a cash distribution or stock offering. But, until then, a lender will usually exclude these types of assets.

Oil and gas interests are complex assets requiring the use of special accounting rules. Like other long-term assets, the basis for accounting for natural resources, such as timber, coal, oil, and gas deposits, is primarily cost. Most likely, any cash investment made by the borrower in an oil and gas venture is or will be amortized as long as the borrower remains vested. Liquidating this interest may be difficult, if not impossible, which is why real estate lenders consider these types of assets worthless.

Time shares are difficult to sell and are usually worth only a fraction of the original cost. Time shares also come with ownership expenses, such as maintenance fees and administrative costs, which lenders would rather do without. Assets such as time shares or vacation co-ops provide little security for the repayment of a loan, which is why lenders overlook this asset, as well.

Goodwill is an intangible asset that represents certain rights and privileges associated with a brand name or franchise. Goodwill is a measure of value in a business in excess of its quantifiable value or identifiable assets tied to cash flow, equipment, machinery, and inventory. Because of the uncertainty involved in estimating the goodwill of a business, goodwill is normally recorded only when a business is acquired by purchase. Lenders regard goodwill as nothing more than a premium, relevant only to the borrower, which is why this asset is dismissed, as well. Other assets ignored by the lender include personal property such as automobiles, boats, guns, art collections, furniture, and jewelry. These assets are rarely liquidated to repay a loan; if they are, they fetch only nickels on the dollar. Confiscating personal property is futile and produces very little cash for the lender.

As illustrated in Figure 3-1, a total of twelve questionable assets were disqualified and excluded from the calculation of net worth. In summary, the overall adjustment by the lender results in a decrease in the sum total of all assets by $3,698,500, which in turn results in an overall decrease in net worth by $3,698,500. Assuming no change in liabilities, net worth declined nearly 50 percent, from $8,000,000 to $4,301,500.

Liabilities in this example are unaffected; in reality, liabilities are rarely adjusted by the lender. The lender's adjustment to the borrower's balance sheet results in a lower net worth of $4,301,500, not the $8,000,000 indicated by the borrower. Since a borrower must have at least a net worth of 50 percent of the loan amount, it is possible that the borrower could get approval for an $8,603,000 real estate loan on the basis of the lender's adjusted net worth valuation of $4,301,500 ($4,301,500 ÷ 0.50 = $8,603,000).

Liquid assets are indicated by asterisks located beside each asset category listed in the short-term asset section of the balance sheet. As illustrated in Figure 3-1, there are seven short-term assets identified as liquid: earnest money deposit, checking accounts, savings accounts, certificates of deposit (CDs), stocks, bonds, and mutual funds. On the basis of these seven assets, total pre-funding liquidity is estimated to be $2,727,000. Assuming a minimum down payment of 20 percent, the borrower will need at least $1.6 million in pre-funding liquidity for an $8 million loan ($8,000,000 × .20 = $1,600,000). The borrower's estimated level of pre-funding liquidity is more than enough to cover the down payment and in fact, exceeds the down payment by $1,127,000 ($2,727,000 − $1,600,000 = $1,127,000). This excess amount of pre-funding liquidity over and above the down payment is the amount available for post-funding liquidity. In this example, post-funding liquidity is estimated to be $1,127,000, which is invested in stocks, bonds, and mutual funds (all of the cash was used for the down payment). As discussed earlier in this section, post-funding liquidity must usually equal either 10 percent of the loan amount or approximately six months' worth of monthly payments of principal and interest. Assuming an interest rate of 6.5 percent and amortization of 30 years, the monthly payment of principal and interest for an $8 million loan would be $50,565; six months' worth of monthly principal and interest payments would be $303,293 ($50,565 × 6 months = $303,392). Ten percent (10%) of the loan amount is $800,000 ($8,000,000 × 0.10 = $800,000). As demonstrated, both estimates are well below the borrower's actual post-funding reserve of $1,127,000. In this example, post-funding liquidity of $1,127,000 exceeds the lender's maximum post-funding liquidity requirement by at least $327,000 ($1,127,000 − $800,000 = $327,000).

Credit Score and History

In years past, commercial real estate lenders paid little or no attention to personal *credit scores* and *payment history*. There was no need to pull a credit report because commercial real estate lenders believed credit risk was limited to the property and its cash flow, not the individual. Commercial mortgages and loans, even to this day, do not usually appear on personal credit reports, which is another reason why lenders tend to overlook credit scores and payment history. Payment history on home mortgages, auto loans, student loans, and credit cards, which are all consumer related, had no influence on a commercial real estate lender's decision concerning commercial mortgages. Today, commercial real estate lenders have become extremely conservative and now believe that personal credit scores and payment history play a significant role in commercial mortgage underwriting.

As previously stated, credit scores in general have not been all that helpful in assessing credit risk concerning commercial mortgages because credit scores are based on consumer, not commercial, loans. Credit scores, often referred to as *FICO* scores, are a reflection of payment history, credit limits, and outstanding balances on home mortgages, installment loans, revolving credit cards, auto loans, and unsecured lines of credit shown on a credit report. FICO is a credit scoring system designed by the Fair Isaac Corporation, hence the acronym. Scores range from a low of 300 to a high of 850. Credit reports are specifically designed for use by consumer lenders, rather than by commercial real estate lenders or commercial lenders in general, for that matter. Even so, commercial real estate lenders are beginning to see the value in credit reports and FICO scores in evaluating credit risk at the borrower or guarantor level. Unlike consumer lenders, commercial real estate lenders do not focus heavily on the credit score itself, unless it is alarmingly low. A FICO score of

600 is low, but not too low to cause a lender to decline a commercial real estate loan. This was especially true for conduit lenders, when they were still originating loans. In general, most commercial real estate lenders look beyond a mediocre or low score as long as there is nothing extremely derogatory shown on the credit report such as numerous late payments in excess of sixty to ninety days, collections, summary judgments, or past bankruptcies. It's also interesting to note, scores usually have no impact on the terms and pricing of commercial real estate loans.

Credit reports and FICO scores pertain to *individuals*, not *borrowing entities*. A borrowing entity is a legal entity such as a partnership, limited liability company, or corporation formed to purchase real estate assets. Borrowing entities can be existing or newly formed. Newly formed entities won't have prior tax filings, financial statements, or credit history. The reason that this distinction between an individual and a borrowing or legal entity is important is that lenders require personal guarantees from individuals, referred to as warm bodies. In other words, lenders look to the individual for the full repayment and guarantee of the indebtedness, not the entity. Legal or borrowing entities created for the sole purpose of owning and operating a single commercial property are referred to as single-asset or special-purpose entities. As the name implies, single-asset entities limit their assets to a single property. There are no other assets whatsoever in a single-asset entity, and, in the absence of an asset such as a commercial property, single-asset entities essentially become shell companies. Guarantees offered by entities, referred to as corporate guarantees, are worthless. In this situation, lenders will require a guarantee from the general and managing partner, assuming that their personal net worth and credit is adequate for repayment of the loan. General partners or managing partners are individuals authorized to run and manage the partnership. In the good old days, general partners or managing members would not give personal guarantees on behalf of the entity, primarily because they owned a very small stake in the partnership and did not want to shoulder 100 percent of the liability. In order to get around the personal guarantee requirement, general and managing partners would search for *nonrecourse loans*. Nonrecourse loans do not require personal guarantees, and, in the event of default, foreclosure is the only option for repayment of the loan. Nevertheless, whether the loan is full recourse or nonrecourse, credit history and credit scores are not to be taken heedlessly.

Five Adverse Credit Conditions Unacceptable to a Commercial Lender

Unlike in years past, credit history and FICO scores today must be nothing short of stellar. The minimum FICO score required for commercial real estate loans depends on the type of loan and varies from lender to lender, but in general a FICO score below 600 is usually where commercial lenders draw the line. Scores below 600 usually mean that a borrower has serious credit problems. Commercial lenders consider scores below 600 unacceptable and therefore usually decline the loan request, no matter how high the borrower's net worth is or how strong the real estate deal may be. If a borrower has a better-than-average score of 650 or higher, many other types of disclosures or even just one *adverse condition* may simply overshadow a good FICO score. Depending on the severity of the adverse condition, it is not unusual for a lender to deny a loan request because of this one adverse condition. These *adverse conditions,* which are all components of a FICO score, are classified into five groups and are listed as follows:

1. Late payment history
2. High credit balances
3. Collections and delinquent accounts

4. Lack of credit

5. Foreclosures, bankruptcies, and summary judgments

Late Payment History

A borrower's *payment history* accounts for 35 percent of his FICO score and is the single most important indication of his ability to make consistent and timely mortgage payments.[1] Experts estimate that a payment that is at least thirty days past due can lower a FICO score by as much as sixty points.[2] Payments that are sixty to ninety days past due really take a toll on a FICO score and may be the sole reason for a lender's decision to decline a commercial real estate loan. Delinquent payments that were thirty, sixty, or ninety days late usually require an explanation from the borrower. Depending on the explanation and extenuating circumstances a lender must ultimately decide whether or not the borrower presents too much risk based on these late payments. Balances that have since been paid in full, even those with numerous late payments in the past, have less and less effect on a borrower's score as time passes. Experts estimate that, on average, past delinquencies that have since been resolved usually lower a score by fifteen to twenty points.[3] However, having other credit lines on which a borrower has always paid on time mitigates the impact of a single missed payment. In summary, the best way for a borrower to ensure that she will not be turned down for a loan is to have a squeaky clean payment history—and that may mean not even one late payment. That may seem impossible, but if a borrower really wants be sure to qualify for that large commercial real estate loan, having a perfect payment history will make all the difference in the world. Late payments are loan killers.

High Credit Balances

A borrower's total *credit balance* accounts for 30 percent of his FICO score and is the second most important indication of his ability to manage debt.[4] High credit card balances, numerous department store credit cards, several automobile and installment loans, all with high balances, spell disaster to a commercial real estate lender. These debts can put a personal strain on a borrower, who may then be tempted to steal or divert cash from the commercial property to keep his personal debt in check. Financial hardship such as this is troublesome to a lender and could put the commercial real estate loan in jeopardy. Credit reports rife with revolving credit card accounts and installment loans can become problematic for the borrower if the aggregate outstanding balance represents a high percentage of the credit limit. Outstanding credit balances are measured as a percentage of the total credit limit. For example, a $5,000 balance on a $10,000 Visa card represents a 50 percent credit balance, which is normally considered too high. Not only does a high percentage of debt to the credit limit reduce a borrower's FICO score, it also sends a signal to a commercial real estate lender that the borrower is overextended and may default during a period of financial hardship. Experts recommend that the balance owed should not exceed 30 percent of the credit limit in order to optimize a FICO score.[5] Borrowers should also refrain from making large purchases within sixty days of applying for a loan in order to keep credit card balances low during the scoring process. If a borrower has too much credit card debt or too many unsecured loans, paying them off in full in one fell swoop can potentially raise a score by seventy points. And, once those credit cards or credit accounts are paid in full, a prospective borrower should keep them open. Closing too many accounts after they have been paid off will reduce the borrower's total credit limit. Decreasing the number of accounts in effect decreases the aggregate credit limit, and, without decreasing debt on accounts that are still open, results in credit balance ratios that remain too high. If a borrower consolidates his debts, it's better to use an installment loan from a bank to pay off revolving debt balances while keeping these revolving accounts open. Installment loans are viewed more favorably by commercial real estate lenders because they show that borrowers can pay off a loan in regular installments over a set period of time, differentiating them from revolving credit cards that seem to have indefinite balances. If a borrower chooses to close a credit card account, it's better to close accounts that are less than two years old. In general, FICO scores are higher for borrowers who have older, active accounts and lower for borrowers with relatively new accounts.

Collections and Delinquent Accounts

Collections and *delinquent accounts* (unpaid accounts that have not yet been turned over to a collection agency) are major red flags for commercial real estate lenders. Collections are a result of failed attempts by the original creditor to collect an outstanding debt. Any account that becomes delinquent or is turned over to a collection agency, no matter how small the debt is, can lower a FICO score by eighty points. So whether it is a $100 medical bill or a $25 cell phone bill, the account is deemed derogatory and negatively impacts the FICO score. Extenuating circumstances that were unavoidable but that resulted in adverse action against the borrower will in most instances be overlooked by a lender if the borrower's explanation is legitimate. However, adverse accounts such as collections that appear to be inexcusable are much more difficult to tolerate. Collections are usually not tolerated unless the borrower is currently disputing an account that has been erroneously turned over to a collection agency. However, lenders feel that there is never an excuse for letting an account morph into a collection no matter who is at fault. No matter how small or large the debt that was turned over for collection, it is still a credit blemish that can tarnish a borrower's creditworthiness. These adverse accounts should be avoided at all costs or expunged from a borrower's credit report as soon as they appear. As time passes, delinquent accounts have less and less impact on a FICO score, so it's paramount to settle the account as soon as possible.

Lack of Credit

A borrower's *credit history* accounts for 15 percent of his FICO score and is the third most important indication of his ability to manage debts responsibly over time.[6] Less is not more when it relates to the number of credit accounts. Having either too few or too many credit card accounts can lower a FICO score. In a sense, when it comes to optimizing a FICO score, it is all about creating the right mix of credit types. If a borrower doesn't have any prior mortgage payment history, for example, it will be very difficult for a commercial real estate lender to assess whether or not the borrower is capable of meeting the monthly mortgage payments. However, even borrowers who are minimalists should consider beefing up their credit history by having at least two to three revolving credit card accounts, a mortgage, and an installment loan, such as an auto loan, or another extension of credit that has been established at least one year. The lender is essentially looking for a lengthy history of monthly payments that demonstrates a borrower's ability to manage a mix of revolving and installment debt. Essentially, the lender will lack confidence in the borrower's ability to pay in a timely manner if the borrower has no history. Borrowers who are debt free but have no credit or payment history should not suddenly open several new credit card accounts all at one time. This approach creates numerous inquiries that can lower a FICO score.

Foreclosures, Bankruptcies, and Summary Judgments

In addition to credit scores, payment history, credit balances, and length of credit history, lenders also look for past *foreclosures, bank-*

ruptcies, and *summary judgments*. A past foreclosure usually means certain death for a borrower. His chance of ever getting loan approval for a new loan is nil, unless there is some mitigating circumstance that could explain the foreclosure. Foreclosures that are at least ten years old may be another exception. As mentioned previously, commercial real estate loans are not listed on a borrower's credit report, so any past commercial mortgage foreclosures will not be immediately obvious to the lender. Other sources such as LexusNexus or UCC filings may disclose foreclosures, but these sources are not reliable. Most borrowers own commercial properties or have the titles to the properties vested in a distinct legal entity such as a limited partnership or corporation. These legal entities can be searched for past foreclosures, as can the borrower's individual name.

Bankruptcies can be either personal or corporate, and the lender will want to know the reason and the nature of the bankruptcy. Credit reports are not supposed to disclose bankruptcies older than ten years or any adverse account information such as collections or outstanding unpaid debts older than seven years. But often bankruptcies are difficult to remove and will stay with the borrower for quite a long time. However, some lenders may allow bankruptcies if they have been fully discharged and are at least seven to ten years old. But any bankruptcies, such as Chapter 7 bankruptcies that are less than seven years old, will be unacceptable to most lenders and will result in denial of credit. In general, before a lender will excuse a bankruptcy, the borrower must demonstrate that he has reestablished good credit from the time of the discharge to the date of the mortgage application. The borrower must also provide in writing a reason for the bankruptcy that is acceptable to the lender.

Summary judgments, *lis pendens*, garnishments, and tax liens must be paid in full or satisfied prior to or concurrent with the loan funding. A summary judgment is an award by the court against the borrower in a case that has not gone to trial. In other words, a summary judgment is an enforceable legal claim for damages or indebtedness against another. *Lis pendens*, Latin for "a suit pending," is a written notice that a lawsuit related to the title to real property or to some interest in real property has been filed. All garnishments and tax liens must be paid in full or removed from a borrower's credit report and from all public records before a lender will fund a loan. Unless these encumbrances are removed, the lender cannot perfect its first lien against the property. Even if they are removed or paid in full to the satisfaction of the lender, the borrower must still furnish a letter of explanation. In summary, summary judgments and liens are headaches that should be dealt with immediately before they show up on a credit report.

Personal Income and Cash Flow

In addition to net worth, liquidity, and good credit, borrowers must have adequate cash flow. There are many terms used to describe *personal cash flow*, such as disposable income, net income, gross income, net cash flow, and free cash flow. *Disposable income* and *net income* both refer to the amount of income or earnings remaining after payment of federal, state, and local taxes, also referred to as "take-home pay" or "after-tax income." *Gross income* refers to the amount of total income or earnings before payment of taxes. *Net cash flow* refers to cash flow or income remaining after payment of mortgage interest and other non-operating expenses associated with real estate investments. *Free cash flow* refers to the amount of gross income remaining after paying living expenses, including payments on home, auto, student, and consumer loans. Financial terms, such as gross income, net income, and the like, can be confusing and may have similar or even double meanings. In fact, the term "free cash flow" may even be new to you or even new to most lenders. But despite its unusual name free cash flow is nothing more than surplus cash that could be used in the event of financial hardship.

Our discussion of free cash flow refers only to a borrower's gross income before income taxes. As illustrated in Figure 3-2, income taxes are not included in the calculation of free cash flow. In our society, when we speak of someone's annual income or salary, we usually mean total earnings before income taxes. The lenders realize that, so, in speaking of personal income and free cash flow, it is not necessary to deduct income taxes. It's important to note that free cash flow should not be confused with disposable income. Disposable income simply refers to after tax income.

Gross Income

Gross income is the sum of all earnings or income from wages, salaries, self-employment, interest, dividends, and net cash flow from rental properties before the payment of federal, state, and local income taxes. A borrower's primary source of income is usually from a salary (for a W-2 employee) or earnings from self-employment. A borrower may also be both a W-2 employee and self-employed through a side business. If a borrower has multiple sources of income, it's important to explain in detail the frequency with which these additional sources of income occur. For example, if a borrower sold an asset such as a fourplex and had a capital gain of $100,000, this income is considered a one-time event. One-time events, such as capital gains, are not considered reliable sources of income and must be excluded in calculating gross income. Often borrowers buy and sell properties for a living and live primarily on the capital gains. In this situation, the capital gains are recurring and relatively reliable. Nevertheless, borrowers must disclose whether or not these sources of income are recurring. If a borrower is a W-2 employee, it is fairly

Figure 3-2. Free Cash Flow.

GROSS INCOME	Annual
Wages and Salary (W-2)	$100,000
Interest and Dividend Income	$15,000
Bonus and Commissions	$25,000
Self-Employment Income	$10,000
Real Estate Income (aggregate net cash flow)	$200,000
Capital Gains (sale of assets)	$150,000
Total Gross Income	$500,000
LESS: EXPENSES (cash only)	
Mortgage (primary residence)	$60,000
Real Estate Taxes and Insurance	$25,000
Utilities	$25,000
Automobile	$15,000
Credit Cards	$6,000
Student Loans	$25,000
Household and Living Expenses	$25,000
Other	$19,000
Total	$200,000
Free Cash Flow	$300,000

safe to assume that his salary is fixed and therefore a reliable source of income. All other sources of income must be verified by pay stubs and tax returns. Large sums of income should be described as either stable, recurring, or one-time events.

In general, borrowers should report only income that is consistent and reliable year after year. As a side note, it is extremely difficult to calculate actual gross income using tax returns because of the inordinate number of deductions, write-offs, and exemptions allowed by the IRS. The process of reconstructing a borrower's true gross income using tax returns is daunting and very time consuming. Often lenders employ or hire a third party to do this analysis for them. Examples of different sources of income include the following:

- Wages and salaries (W-2)
- Bonuses and commissions
- Interest and dividends
- Business income (self-employment)
- Capital gains
- Rental income
- Partnerships and joint ventures
- Trusts
- Oil and gas royalties
- Alimony and child support
- Annuities and retirement distributions
- Social Security

Self-Employment Income

Borrowers who are self-employed are scrutinized more carefully than borrowers who have stable salaried jobs. A lender will need a brief description of the type of business the borrower owns and its history of revenue. In addition to business financial statements, the lender will require a complete set of income tax returns for at least the three most recent years of operations. Gross income from self-employment usually includes ordinary income or profit from the borrower's primary business and investment income generated from rental properties. In some cases, a borrower's self-employment business may consist solely of the ownership and management of commercial real estate. In this type of sole proprietorship, the borrower's personal or gross income is derived from the net cash flow from the ownership of real estate. In either situation, a lender will need to compare the borrower's business income statement with the income tax returns for that same calendar year. The borrower's business income statement will have to be reconciled with the income tax returns. If the business income statements differ significantly from the tax returns, the tax returns will always supersede. Occasionally, lenders will order transcripts from the IRS and discover that income tax returns given to the lender do not match the returns actually filed with the IRS. A transcript is a computerized version of the signed tax return filed with the IRS with all its schedules, referred to as IRS Form 4506-T. If the transcript is different from the returns that the borrower claims to have sent to the IRS, the lender may suspect fraud and decline the loan immediately.

Net Cash Flow and Taxable Net Cash Flow from Rental Income

Net cash flow specifically refers to income derived from real estate investments such as single-family and commercial properties. Net cash flow can be the borrower's sole income, or it can be additional income that is added to a borrower's primary income such as a salary. Anytime a significant portion of *gross income* is coming from aggregate net cash flow (refer to Figure 3-2), it's usually a pretty good indication the borrowers are professional real estate investors engaged full time in the real estate business. Net cash flow is not to be con-fused with *net operating income* (NOI). As discussed in Chapter 2, net operating income is cash flow available *before* debt service and is not passed through to the owner, at least not yet. Net cash flow, on the other hand, is cash flow available *after* debt service. Net cash flow, assuming it represents a profit, is the income from a rental property that is finally passed through to the owner. As illustrated in Figure 3-3a, net cash flow is simply calculated by subtracting *nonoperating expenses* from the property's NOI, such as mortgage interest, legal and professional fees, and administrative and management fees associated with the partnership. *Nonoperating expenses* are actual costs that are not integral to the operation of the property, also referred to as *below-the-line expenses. Operating expenses* and *nonoperating expenses* alike are *cash expenses. Cash expense* are those expenses or costs that require an actual outlay of cash. A *noncash expense*, such as depreciation and amortization, is a cost that does not involve an actual outlay of cash and is only an accounting adjustment used in preparing financial statements and tax returns. Subtracting noncash expenses from net cash flow, such as depreciation and amortization, results in a *taxable net cash flow.* Net cash flow can also be used to calculate a borrower's return on equity, also referred to as cash-on-cash return.

Taxable net cash flow is calculated strictly for the purpose of reducing a borrower's tax liability. As illustrated in Figure 3-3a, depreciation and amortization, for example, are noncash expenses that reduce a borrower's net cash flow from $15,000 to $5,000. In this example the borrower actually earns $15,000, but only pays taxes on $5,000. Lenders are fully aware of these noncash expenses and take them into account when calculating the borrower's actual net cash flow. Figure 3-3a illustrates the calculation of and the difference between net cash flow and taxable net cash flow.

Figure 3-3a. Net Cash Flow vs. Taxable Net Cash Flow.

	Net Cash Flow	Taxable Net Cash Flow
Net Operating Income (NOI)	$100,000	$100,000
LESS: Cash Expenses:		
Mortgage Interest	($80,000)	($80,000)
Administrative	($1,000)	($1,000)
Asset Mgmt. Fee	($3,000)	($3,000)
Auto/Travel	($1,000)	($1,000)
Net Cash Flow	$15,000	$15,000
LESS: Noncash Expenses:		
Depreciation		($8,000)
Amortization		($2,000)
Taxable Net Cash Flow		$5,000

Aggregate net cash flow from real estate income, as shown in Figure 3-2, is a sum of the net cash flow from each and every real estate investment or income-producing property within a borrower's portfolio. However, it is important to note that the total income or loss shown on the borrower's tax return (Form 1040, Schedule E) is actually the aggregate taxable net cash flow, which is most often a negative number or in other words shown as a loss instead of positive income. Lenders are fully aware of this issue and often just add back depreciation and amortization to the aggregate taxable net cash flow in order to calculate or re-establish a borrower's true aggregate net cash flow.

For example, if taxable net cash flow (same as "income" or "loss" on page 1 of Schedule E) for a single investment property is $5,000, and depreciation and amortization expenses are $8,000 and $2,000, respectively, net cash flow can be simply calculated by adding $8,000 and $2,000 back to taxable net cash flow. Figure 3-3b illustrates how taxable net cash flow is converted back to net cash flow.

But more often than not, a borrower will own a dozen or more properties vested in a dozen or more partnerships, which in turn creates a convoluted web of tax returns too complicated to comprehend. Despite this reality, some lenders will forge ahead anyway, no matter how complicated tax returns may be. However, many lenders prefer to use a much faster, if not easier, method in calculating aggregate net cash flow. Instead of using tax returns or financial statements (which are really one and the same, since accountants use the financial statements to prepare the tax returns), a lender will use an Excel spreadsheet, referred to as a *Real Estate Owned Schedule* (REO Schedule). This method is discussed in greater depth in Chapter 5.

Figure 3-3b. Net Cash Flow vs. Taxable Net Cash Flow.

Reverse Calculation of Net Cash Flow	
Taxable Net Cash Flow	$5,000
(same as "income" or "loss" page 1 of Schedule E)	
ADD: Non-Cash Expenses	
Depreciation	$8,000
Amortization	<u>$2,000</u>
Net Cash Flow	$15,000

Cash Flow Statement

As mentioned earlier, *free cash flow* is the monthly or annual amount of gross income remaining after paying living expenses, including payments on home, auto, student, and other types of installment loans. Free cash flow is usually calculated using a *cash flow statement,* such as the one illustrated in Figure 3-4. The cash flow statement looks very similar to a business income and expense statement except that the income section is referred to as "sources of cash" and the expense section is referred to as "uses of cash." A cash flow statement pertains to personal cash inflows and cash outflows only, unlike a typical business or property income and expense statement, which uses an accrual accounting method that includes both cash and noncash income and expenses. There are business cash flow statements prepared by CPAs, and there are personal cash flow statements prepared by individuals. Lenders prefer personal cash flow statements, similar to the one illustrated in Figure 3-4. Preparing an accurate and truthful cash flow statement can take hours or even days, and the statements are often inaccurate and incomplete. The integrity of a personal cash flow statement is dependent on the honesty of the borrower. In order to pinpoint any discrepancies, lenders often compare the total amount of personal debts listed on the borrower's cash flow statement to the total amount of debts reported on the credit report. If a discrepancy is found, borrowers must either correct the mistake or provide an explanation. Lenders can often verify income reported on a cash flow statement using tax returns but the same does not hold true for expenses. With the exception of mortgages, auto loans, and credit cards, which can be verified using a credit report, household and living expenses are merely estimates. A cash flow statement should always be signed, dated, and certified by the borrower. A cash flow statement that is certified is one that has been authenticated and represents a true, complete, and correct statement of financial condition.

Figure 3-4. Cash Flow Statement.

CASH FLOW STATEMENT

Please provide the following information regarding sources and uses of cash during the calendar year and your projections for the current year. If a cash flow deficit exists, explain how the existing or requested debt will be serviced. Income from alimony, child support, or maintenance payments need not be revealed unless you wish to have them considered as a basis for repaying the requested credit.

Individual ( ) Joint ( )	Prior Year	Current Estimate
SOURCES OF CASH		
1. Gross wages or salaries		
2. Bonuses, commissions, etc.		
3. Rental income		
4. Interest and dividend income		
5. Sale of assets		
6. Distributions from estates and trusts		
7. Distributions from businesses, partnerships, or joint ventures		
8. Income tax refund		
9. Other sources of cash		
TOTAL CASH RECEIVED		
USES OF CASH		
1. Homestead mortgage payments		
2. Rental mortgage payments		
3. Bank loans—principal and interest		
4. Other loans—principal and interest		
5. Rental expenses		
6. Real estate taxes		
7. Living expenses (utilities, rent, insurance, household, etc.)		
8. Other uses of cash		
TOTAL CASH OUTLAYS		
NET CASH FLOW		

CASH FLOW SURPLUS (DEFICIT)

The undersigned certifies that the information presented on this cash flow and personal financial statement has been carefully read and is a true, complete, and correct statement of my (our) financial condition as of the date shown and does not omit any pertinent information.
I (We) understand that misrepresenting information on this (or any attachments) statement is a criminal offense under federal law.

Date:_____   Signed_____

                          Signed_____

Banking and
Credit References

A *banking* or *credit reference* is very much like a referral. Banks in general are usually cooperative and willing to vouch for an existing customer. Information released to a prospective lender by a bank with whom a borrower has an existing relationship is very limited. Banks usually do not need prior approval from the customer before releasing such information to a prospective lender. A credit or bank reference can either be oral or written. An oral reference is nothing more than a telephone interview. A telephone interview can expose personality traits about the borrower such as commitment, character, integrity, motivation, and attitudes about debt that cannot otherwise be detected through the normal back-office underwriting and credit analysis. A bad reference, believe it or not, in spite of ample liquidity, an impressive net worth, years of experience, and a high credit score, may still result in denial of credit. Therefore, do not offer as references potential problem creditors or disgruntled bankers that might be antagonistic or negative toward the borrower.

A *written reference*, commonly referred to as a "bank letter of reference," is a one-page letter written and addressed to the prospective lender. The letter is nothing more than a validation of the borrower's creditworthiness and good standing. A second type of written reference, which can be used in lieu of a letter, is a standard bank form referred to as a *verification of mortgage* (VOM). A VOM is a one-page document that a bank, creditor, or mortgage company completes on behalf of a borrower. Information on a VOM is limited to a loan's status, payment history and balance, and maybe a few comments. VOMs are common with large retail banks that do not feel comfortable writing a personal letter of reference. For fear of a lawsuit, credit policies often prohibit loan officers from making written statements concerning a borrower's credit without approval from senior management. In this situation, the best that a prospective lender can hope for in terms of a written reference is a VOM.

Whether oral or written, an excellent credit reference or a good word by a fellow banker can carry a lot of weight, so it's important for borrowers to stay in the good graces of their bankers and loan officers. Loan officers do not like problem borrowers, so borrowers who pay on time and perform according to the loan covenants make banks and lenders very happy. Each successful transaction builds upon the preceding one; therefore, it's important that business relations between banker and borrower remain solid. A borrower who is rude and demanding can ruin a banking relationship. A good reference should be one that not only commends a borrower's ability to perform but also praises his character and professionalism.

A bank and credit reference should include more than just a bank name and telephone number. It should also include an address, contact person, loan account number, length of banking relationship, beginning credit limit, current lending limit, number of outstanding loans, type of loan, current balances, maturity dates, and a list of past and current transactions. A sample banking and credit reference is shown in Figure 3-5.

Notes

1. www.myfico.com/CreditEducation/FactFallacies.aspx. "Understanding Your FICO Score" (pdf booklet for download).
2. Ibid.
3. Ibid.
4. Ibid.
5. Ibid.
6. Ibid.

Figure 3-5. Banking and Credit Reference.

Bank:	First National Bank
Address:	1000 Main Street, Houston, Texas 77002
Contact:	John Smith, VP of Commercial Real Estate Lending
Phone:	555-250-1900
Length of Banking Relationship:	5 Years
Beginning Lending Limit:	$1,000,000
Current Lending Limit:	$6,000,000
Outstanding Loan Balances:	$4,000,000
Past Transactions:	$800,000 Construction loan for a Retail Center, Houston, TX
	$1,000,000 Bridge loan for the acquisition of a 10,000-SF office building, Houston, TX
	$2,500,000 Permanent fixed-rate loan for the purchase of an 80-unit apartment complex, Galveston, TX
Current Transactions:	$3,500,000 Construction loan for a 100-unit apartment complex, Conroe, TX
	$1,000,000 Renovation bridge loan for a 10,000-SF retail center, Friendswood, TX
	$1,500,000 Permanent fixed-rate loan for a 15,000-SF office building, Houston, TX
	$2,000,000 Line of Credit

CHAPTER 4

REAL ESTATE EXPERIENCE

Commercial real estate investing involves more than just managing cash flow; it requires asset know-how, talent, and years of real hands-on experience. There are two types of experience relevant to commercial real estate: *ownership* and *management*. Ownership and management are entirely two different disciplines; however, if one is experienced in management, it is safe to conclude that one is qualified in ownership. But the same assumption does not hold true for ownership. If one is experienced in owning and investing in commercial real estate, it cannot be assumed that one is also qualified in management.

Ownership and Management Experience

Experience in the *ownership* and *management* of commercial real estate is paramount in any transaction and can never be over-emphasized. If a borrower has no prior experience managing commercial real estate or, worse yet, has never owned commercial real estate at any time in her career, the odds that she will find a loan will not be in her favor. In the eyes of a lender, an inexperienced borrower with a high net worth is just as risky as an experienced borrower with no net worth at all. Lenders want borrowers who have experience, plain and simple. In some circumstances, a mediocre or average net worth or credit score may be excused if a borrower has years of experience and a successful track record, but it is rare. Whenever experience trumps a weak balance sheet, it usually means that there are favorable mitigating circumstances, such as pent-up demand, an excellent location, rising market values, and a healthy local economy. These kinds of favorable market conditions are considered on a case-by-case basis. However, bear in mind that such cases are the exception, not the rule.

Ownership Experience

Owning and operating a single-family investment property, such as a duplex or fourplex, do not make a borrower automatically qualified for a commercial real estate loan. Investing in commercial real estate is a complicated and time-consuming endeavor that is both capital and management intensive. Unfortunately, single-family investors who try to transition from single-family investing to commercial often bite off more than they can chew and find themselves overwhelmed or at risk of losing the property. For that reason, a borrower must be able to demonstrate to a banker that he has prior relevant commercial experience. The easiest way of demonstrating that is by providing the banker with a list of real estate assets, referred to as an *REO Schedule*. An REO Schedule, which stands for "real estate owned," is a list of real property, both single-family and commercial, owned by the borrower. This list or schedule, which is discussed in Chapter 5, makes it obvious to the banker that the borrower has current and/or prior experience purchasing, owning, and operating commercial real estate. Owning several tracts of vacant land or several residential lots and nothing more is an example of weak ownership experience. Bankers are really looking for borrowers who can demonstrate solid and sound experience owning and operating commercial-size income-producing properties that require extensive management.

On the other hand, a real estate portfolio with nothing more than a single-family home may be misleading at first glance. In other words, the current size of a borrower's portfolio is not necessarily an indication of a lack of experience. Often borrowers will cash out by selling off their entire portfolio over time if they feel it's time to exit the market for a while. If that is the case, and it happens quite often, a written narrative or explanation describing prior ownership experience is highly recommended. This written narrative should include a list of projects and properties purchased and sold over the years with details such as type of property, number of units, square feet, address, purchase date, sale date, purchase price, cost of capital improvements and renovations, name of contractor, name of property management company, and sales price.

Ownership to a lender is more than just collecting rents at the first of the month. It involves active participation in everyday operations, such as marketing vacant space, optimizing rent, reducing turnover, minimizing overhead and operating costs, and making capital improvements. Professional management companies can do all these things, but rarely do they do them in a cost-effective way. Their objective, just like that of any other business, is to increase volume and maximize revenue, usually at the expense of the property owner. However, it needs to be emphasized that the kind of active ownership participation mentioned here is not about one's property management skills; it's about one's competence in dealing with a hired professional management company. Lenders actually prefer that borrowers hire third-party professional management companies, but that doesn't mean that a lender will excuse a borrower's lack of experience. Lenders that frequently hear prospective borrowers say that "they will just hire a management company to take of the property" see this as a red flag. Because of a statement like that, a lender may wonder if the borrower is truly inexperienced or just plain naive. Borrowers who are naive put too much trust in third-party management companies and believe that they do not have to make any decisions. A passive or absent owner can lead to complacency and mismanagement. It is for this very reason that many passive borrowers and investors find themselves losing control of the property.

Prior ownership experience means not only knowing how to physically operate the building but also knowing how to interface and communicate with the management company. Owners or landlords can be so frugal and controlling that they effectively reduce the management company to nothing more than a bookkeeper. Successful owners know how to find the right balance between management and control. A borrower must also know how to read and interpret the management company's financial statements. Without this experience, a borrower can be robbed blind and not even know it. So, ownership experience is more than just showing the banker the deed to the property; it involves a whole lot more skill than one thinks. A borrower who has sufficient ownership experience should be able to say that she has encountered the following situations or aspects of ownership at one time or another in her career. In other words, an experienced owner of commercial real estate should know how to:

- ➤ Select and hire property management companies
- ➤ Select and hire leasing and marketing specialists
- ➤ Select and hire general contractors
- ➤ Prepare and execute tenant leases
- ➤ Prepare and negotiate tenant improvement allowances
- ➤ Renovate or repair commercial buildings
- ➤ Select and contract with suppliers and commercial vendors
- ➤ Advertise and lease vacant space
- ➤ Create and prepare financial reports (e.g., rent rolls, P&Ls)
- ➤ Use real estate accounting software
- ➤ Handle tenant disputes and evictions

Management Experience

Commercial properties are either self-managed or managed by a professional management company hired by the borrower. The kind of *management* experience we are referring to is *on-site property management* experience, such as managing a staff of employees, handling leasing and marketing, and dealing with repair and maintenance requests. Borrowers who manage their own properties are referred to as *owner-managers.* Owner-managers are common among investors in small commercial or multifamily properties who live out-of-state and have to depend on others who are usually part-time employees or family friends. Owner-managers are quite capable of managing larger investment properties, as well. However, managing a commercial property is no easy feat and can often be more trouble than it's worth. Many owner-managers who start off managing their own properties learn soon enough how complicated and nerve-racking it can be. It's not to say that owner-managers are incapable of managing their own properties. The question is whether they are managing the properties efficiently. Management experience is not cut and dried, though many professional management companies would argue differently. Lenders are frequently skeptical of owner-managers, unless they can be persuaded otherwise. The decision about whether an owner-manager will be required to hire a third-party professional management company is really at the discretion of the lender.

The extent of an owner-manager's management experience depends on many factors such as length of ownership, leasing and marketing skills, size of staff, occupancy history, physical condition of properties, and record of health and safety compliance. It shouldn't be assumed that simply managing a half-dozen properties for the past five years automatically makes anyone a competent management company. Final judgment concerning management experience may even be withheld until a banker has had a chance to conduct a drive-by inspection of the properties. Drive-by inspections are a way for lenders to get a firsthand look at the kind of job the borrower has been doing. An impressive and slick company resumé indicating twenty or even thirty years of management experience will simply be an object of scorn if the borrower turns out to be a slumlord. Borrowers who boast of their management prowess will have to prove it beyond a shadow of a doubt because lenders are not so easily convinced. Whether or not a borrower is presumed capable of managing his or her property, the burden of proof is never the lender's responsibility. Lenders in general are not all that keen on borrowers who try to self-manage, and those that insist on self-managing do so at the risk of having their loan request denied. Borrowers who can successfully demonstrate property management skills equal to those of a professional third-party management company are usually the exception, not the rule. Occasionally, lenders will back down and waive the professional management company requirement. If they do, it's because the borrower presented a very persuasive argument for self-management. Persuading a lender to waive the professional management company requirement is no easy task and requires a lot of details. If you think a one-page company resumé will do the trick, think again. Lenders like stories, especially success stories, which only narratives can convey. A list of the names and locations of current and past properties under management says nothing. A persuasive narrative chronicles and recounts purchase dates, purchase prices, repairs, renovations, turnover ratios, occupancy history, profits, growth as well as personal involvement and past employment. A narrative should be anecdotal because that's the only way a lender can be convinced.

The following narrative is an example of a very persuasive presentation describing the borrower's experience in both ownership and management. This narrative is an excerpt taken from an actual credit memorandum prepared for the chief credit officer of a commercial bank that had previously denied not only the borrower's request to self-manage but the loan request, as well. The loan request was for the purchase of an apartment complex with 138 units, much larger than anything the borrower had ever owned and managed before. Initially, the borrower was deemed inexperienced because of his lack of current and historical ownership in a comparable property. In other words, the borrower had no previous experience in owning and managing a large apartment complex. In fact, the only commercial property within the borrower's portfolio at the time was a small twelve-unit apartment complex. A portfolio of this size and caliber was not acceptable. To be considered acceptable in this situation, the portfolio should have included at least three or four apartment complexes no smaller than fifty units in size. To judge from the borrower's REO Schedule alone, it would seem that the borrower was indeed inexperienced, but if one dug deeper, this rush to judgment seemed premature. As a result of this persuasive narrative, however, the chief credit officer effectively reversed his earlier decision and approved the loan. Before providing this narrative, the borrowers had been deemed inexperienced and incapable of handling a larger property such as the one they had under contract.

JOHN AND JANE DOE'S OWNERSHIP AND MANAGEMENT EXPERIENCE

John and Jane Doe are a husband and wife team. They have been purchasing and renovating single-family and multifamily properties for 26 years. Their company is called Apartment Assets Corp. Mr. Doe is 43 years old and is originally from Italy and moved to the US twenty years ago. Mr. Doe has always been self-employed in the real estate business. He began his real estate career buying and refurbishing homes in the Atlanta area during the early 1980s. He eventually graduated up to 8-plexes and smaller 12-unit apartment complexes throughout Atlanta. They eventually moved down to Florida seven years ago and have been buying land, apartment projects, and building multiple-unit condo projects from the ground up.

Mr. Doe's current real estate portfolio is valued at $7,135,000 and includes the following properties:

- A 12-unit condo project in Fort Myers, FL, that they built from the ground up that is now a 100% rental project that they manage

- Five rental properties composed of four single-family homes and one condo

- Eight-lot multifamily parcel that is zoned for a maximum of twelve units, Miami, FL (future MF or condo project)

- Ten-lot multifamily parcel that is zoned for a maximum of twelve units, Orlando, FL (future MF or condo project)

- Four-lot multifamily parcel that is zoned for a maximum of twenty units, Jupiter, FL (future MF or condo project)

> Six contiguous lots for the development of one single-family home (ocean frontage)

> Two contiguous lots for the development of one single-family home (ocean frontage)

Following is a description of their past projects, which have since been sold:

> A 54-unit apartment complex, Fort Myers, FL (SOLD)

This was their first large apartment purchase when they moved to Florida. They bought the property for $1,100,000 and spent $400,000 on renovations and capital improvements. The project was 100% occupied but with riff-raff, drug dealers, and undesirables. Within months they were able to clean out the bad tenants and re-tenant the property with hard-working blue-collar residents. They managed the property for 6 years and eventually sold it in Nov 2006 for $4.4 million realizing a $2.8 million profit.

> A 12 unit condominium project, Jacksonville, FL (SOLD)

This project was a ground-up construction of a two-story, 12-unit condominium project that they developed themselves and managed the HOA until all of the units were sold and then they turned over the management of the HOA to the homeowners. These units completely sold out. They completed a second 12-unit condominium project (listed above) that they still own due to the fallout of the condo market. They decided to keep it and convert it to a rental community.

The borrowers plan on developing the multifamily parcels in the future. They clearly have many years of experience in

multifamily management and tenant-to-landlord relations. The
subject property that they intend to buy is 138 units comprised
of ten (10) buildings. There is no swimming pool and the
buildings are very basic and 95% occupied with primarily blue-
collar families. The loan officer asked why the borrower wanted
to buy a property in Dallas instead of staying in Florida. The
borrower replied, "Cap rates are too low in Florida and that the
price per unit for this property is a bargain."

Mr. Doe currently employs his cousin in Florida and will relocate
him to the Dallas property to be the full-time on-site manager.
Mr. Doe uses multifamily management software called Tenant
Pro to manage his properties. He plans to spend one week each
month during the first year at the property until he completes
the training of the on-site manager, and maintenance personnel
and completes the renovations that he has planned for the
property. He wants to repaint the entire exterior and install
surveillance cameras. The loan officer inspected the property
and it is a basic 10-building apartment complex that does not
present any challenges. There is no pool or any other
maintenance-intensive or personnel-intensive activities at the
property. The complex is located not far from where the bank's
regional manager lives and fronts University Blvd., an extremely
busy road in the inner-city area of Dallas where land values are
skyrocketing.

The borrowers clearly have relevant experience and the fact that
they are out-of-state is not that problematic. Mr. Doe is self-
employed and has never worked for anybody other than for
himself for his real estate business. He has no other projects or
obligations that would interfere with his ability to efficiently
manage this 95% occupied property. He has created
Homeowners Associations for his condo projects and has

managed hundreds of apartments during his 26-year career as a real estate investor.

The next example is a narrative describing a borrower's experience in property management. In this case, the borrowers' ownership experience was not in question; it was their ability to self-manage the property that was in doubt. The borrowers were primarily single-family-home builders who built and invested in duplexes. They were also owner-managers of their entire portfolio. Again, like that of the married couple in the previous example, the size of their REO portfolio was unimpressive. Essentially, there was no indication whatsoever of any property management experience. Without an explanation or further convincing, a lender would simply decline a borrower's request to self-manage. It took some extra research and probing to uncover the fact that the borrowers did indeed have the experience and the track record to successfully manage their own properties. The following narrative is an excerpt from an actual credit memorandum presented to a chief credit offer for approval that yet again resulted in waiving the third-party management company requirement.

JOE SMITH AND JOHN BROWN'S MANAGEMENT EXPERIENCE AND MANAGEMENT PLAN

Borrowers Joe Smith and John Brown are local residents of Hallsville, Texas, which is located 6 miles east of Longview, Texas, and 20 miles west of Marshall, Texas. They have been partners in building and investing in single-family and multifamily rental homes for 6 years. Their current portfolio includes a total of 27 rental units comprised of five (5) single-family rentals, four (4) duplexes, two (2) triplexes and two (2) four-duplexes. Their management company ABC Management employs a full-time manager named Mary White. Ms. White's duties include collecting monthly rent, marketing and advertising in local publications such "Apartment Finder.com," screening potential tenants, scheduling and coordinating maintenance and repair requests, and general bookkeeping.

The borrowers belong to the Texas Apartment Association (TAA), which provides landlord support for tenant relations and serves as the official state organization for landlord rights and legal remedies, such as eviction procedures. TAA is the single largest provider for lease forms and legal documents as well as legal counsel for landlords throughout Texas. Applicant processing is done by a third-party company called Tenant Tracker, located in McKinney, TX. They process the landlord's tenant application for a $25 fee, which includes a complete credit and income check including verification of previous rental and mortgage history. Tenant Tracker also verifies the applicant's income by calling the employer and faxing the forms on behalf of the landlord. They also run criminal background checks. Tenant Tracker faxes all this information back to the landlord. The applicant's monthly income must be 3 times the monthly rent and requires a $300 security deposit. If the applicant's income is less than 3 times the monthly rent then the applicant is required to pay in advance a security deposit in the amount of one full month's rent plus $300.

The Hallsville duplexes, which are located right next to the brand new duplexes and triplexes that Joe Smith has recently built, can be easily managed by the borrowers since they live and own their businesses right in Hallsville (Longview), TX. The seller of the Hallsville duplexes currently employs a full-time maintenance supervisor named Kevin Ball, who lives in Unit A on Woodridge Circle. Mr. Ball has been employed at the property for 16 years with an annual salary of $52,000. The borrowers plan on retaining Mr. Ball as their lead maintenance supervisor upon acquisition of the properties. Mr. Ball will continue to maintain the duplexes in Hallsville but will take on new responsibilities at the Marshall duplexes as well. Mr. Ball is a certified AC technician and handles all other repairs as they are needed including all make-ready work, cleaning, and painting. Carpet cleaning, lawn care, and carpet replacement are all contracted out. The seller currently self-manages both the Hallsville and Marshall duplexes. Unit B on Navajo Trail in Marshall is used as the full-time leasing and management office where tenants can pay their rent and make repair requests. The management office is also stocked with parts and maintenance supplies such as light bulbs, air filters, locks, etc. Mary White will be working out of this office as the full-time on-site manager. All utilities are paid by the tenants with the exception of trash service, which is paid by the landlord. Other than the items mentioned above there is essentially very little to manage at these duplexes.

Both narratives present examples of borrowers who, because of their unimpressive REO Schedules, appeared to be either inexperienced in both ownership and management or just strictly inexperienced in property management. Nevertheless, they were both small, part-time real estate investors trying to expand their portfolios without the help of professionals. Borrowers and mortgage brokers must view the lender as a customer or client to whom they are trying to sell some-thing; what they are trying to sell is their ability to successfully and competently own and operate the property, which in turn provides the cash flow to pay back the loan. Time and time again borrowers and mortgage brokers fail to take the time to prepare these narratives or resumés and then are surprised when their loan request is declined. This section of the loan request package is often neglected or missing altogether. It cannot be emphasized enough that a lender needs to be persuaded if it is not obvious that there are professionals involved in the transaction. Otherwise, the lender will automatically presume that it is dealing with an amateur. Don't leave any doubt in the lender's mind, and be prepared for questions. There is no such thing as too much information regarding a borrower's experience. Take the time to interview the borrower as though he were applying for a job and write down and summarize for the lender each and every qualification. This may take a lot of time and work, but when the loan closes, the effort will not have been in vain.

CHAPTER 5

REAL ESTATE ASSETS

As illustrated in Chapter 3, the asset side of a balance sheet includes both current (short-term) assets and fixed (long-term) assets. Examples of fixed assets include land, buildings, equipment, furniture, fixtures, or just real estate in general. The values of a fixed asset such as real estate is often shown as a lump sum or aggregate number simply because there is little room on a one-page balance sheet to list each and every property. Likewise, the total balance of all outstanding mortgages corresponding to each and every property is a lump sum shown on the liability side of the balance sheet. It is for this reason that a separate real estate schedule is required. Lenders often refer to this type of schedule as a *Schedule of Real Estate Owned* or *REO Schedule*. This schedule is designed to represent the borrower's entire *real estate portfolio*. The word "portfolio" is merely vernacular for the word "schedule." The significance and weight of an REO Schedule cannot be overemphasized. After the balance sheet, it is the single most important document a lender uses in underwriting the borrower. The REO Schedule essentially provides specific details that a balance sheet cannot, and without it underwriting of the loan may simply come to a halt.

The REO Schedule

As discussed in Chapter 4, the degree of ownership and management experience, as a rule, is a function of the quantity, quality, and complexity of properties that constitute a real estate portfolio. In the absence of a company resumé, a seasoned commercial lender can sometimes discern whether or not the borrower has adequate ownership or management experience simply by scrutinizing the borrower's real estate portfolio. A preliminary review of the portfolio or schedule by an experienced underwriter can also indicate whether the borrower is a large corporate real estate company, a seasoned individual investor, or merely an amateur.

Lenders prefer that borrowers list all of their properties within their portfolios on a document referred to as a *Schedule of Real Estate Owned* or *REO Schedule*, for short. The REO Schedule is a fairly standard bank form used by most commercial real estate lenders. However, many of the standard REO Schedules floating around out there are considered inadequate and ask for only about half the information usually needed by underwriters. Underwriting commercial real estate loans is more of an art than a science, which may be the main reason that REO Schedules are not all alike. The average REO Schedule includes basic information such as property name, address, property type, market value, existing loan balance, monthly income, and monthly expenses, but it is the level of detail that distinguishes a superior schedule from an inferior one. For example, some REO Schedules do not provide columns or spaces to input the property's acquisition date, the borrower's percentage of ownership interest, or even the property's monthly operating expenses. The fact that REO Schedules are not identical doesn't mean that any one particular REO Schedule is better than another; it's just that some schedules are considered less useful than others. A proficient and useful REO Schedule has the right mix of columns, rows, and blanks to be filled in by the borrower all on one page, thus providing a clear and concise picture of the borrower's real estate assets. In order to create an REO Schedule considered acceptable by just about every lender, it's important to first understand its anatomy and structure. The remainder of this chapter will show you how to create an REO Schedule, and will discuss in detail its anatomy, layout, and meaning, and the relevance of each column heading.

The REO Schedule and the Balance Sheet

As previously mentioned, the lump sum or aggregate value of all real estate assets listed in the fixed (long-term) assets section of the balance sheet must be supported by the REO Schedule. It is also important to note that the lump sum or aggregate value shown on the balance sheet must be identical to the sum total value of all properties listed on the REO Schedule. The presumption here is that the borrower has multiple properties too numerous to fit within a single space on the balance sheet, thus requiring a separate REO Schedule. If a borrower owns only one or two properties, then most likely he will individually list these properties directly on the balance sheet and omit the REO Schedule altogether. However, this method is often not practical, since many borrowers own multiple, if not, dozens, of properties. Borrowers are faced with the same problem using standard fill-in-the-blank bank forms provided by banks. The most common type of fill-in-the-blank form available at any bank is a two- to three-page consolidated balance sheet and statement of income and expenses, referred to as the personal financial statement. This form is designed for borrowers who do not already have their own set of personal financial statements, though its use is optional. These forms are available mainly as a courtesy or convenience in case a borrower needs assistance. Personal financial statements prepared by the borrower or the borrower's accountant are perfectly acceptable and are often attached to the blank form in lieu of completing the bank's version. When borrowers have their own set of personal financial statements, banks often require that they sign and date the bank's version anyway.

To avoid any confusion, it is important to restate that the personal financial statement comprises three main financial documents: a balance sheet, an income statement, and a cash flow statement. With regard to the REO Schedule, the only financial document of concern for the purpose of this discussion is the balance sheet. In general, personal financial statements used by loan applicants (the fill-in-the-blank form provided by banks) differ from bank to bank. These generic bank forms provide little room or space to input information and can often be confusing. Within these different personal financial statements, balance sheets can vary in design and layout. However, in spite of the different versions floating around out there, there is at least one constant, and that is that all balance sheets allocate no more than a single space or line for each asset category. Occasionally, a balance sheet may provide several spaces or lines where borrowers can list other or miscellaneous assets not already preprinted on the form. Nevertheless, there is at least one space allocated for each asset's total value.

Figure 5-1 and Figure 5-2 are examples of two different types of balance sheets with different layouts but with similar single-space formats. In other words, although the balance sheets are laid out differently, they both provide only a single space or box for each asset's total value. As illustrated in Figure 5-1, the asset section of the balance sheet found on page 2 of any Fannie Mae Form 1003 allocates only a single box in which to enter the total value for each asset category (e.g., cash, marketable securities, real estate). Fannie Mae Form 1003, a residential loan application titled *Uniform Residential Loan Application*, is used quite often for small commercial real estate loan requests. This standard form is an all-in-one loan application and personal financial statement that includes both a balance sheet and income and expense statement.

Figure 5-2 is an example of a different type of balance sheet that uses a single-space format similar to the balance sheet section of the Fannie Mae Form 1003 illustrated in Figure 5-1. As illustrated in

Figure 5-1. Asset Column of Section VI, "Assets and Liabilities," Page 2 of Fannie Mae Form 1003.

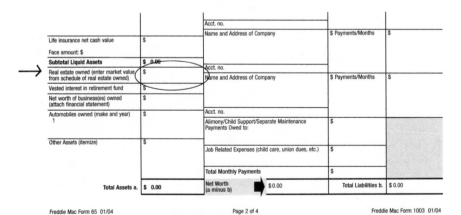

Figure 5-2, the asset section of the balance sheet (Section A) on the first page of a generic bank form (a bank fill-in-the-blank version) allocates only a single space or box in which to enter the total value for real estate or any other non–real estate asset. However, in this example there is a slight difference in that there is a separate line for the loan applicant's homestead.

A second constant among different types of balance sheets, in addition to the single-space or single-line format, is the reference to a schedule. For example, in Figure 5-1 the real estate line includes a parenthetical note that reads "enter market value from schedule of real estate owned." The real estate line in Figure 5-2 includes a parenthetical note that reads "Schedule 6." These schedules provide the details and individual values from which the total value was derived. So far, the consistency among different balance sheets has been limited to the single-space format and the reference to a schedule found within their asset sections. But what about the schedules? Are these REO Schedules, associated with the different balance sheets, consis-

Figure 5-2. Asset Column of Section A, Page 1 of a Generic Bank Form.

SECTION A: ASSETS

CASH	(Schedule 1)		401,659
MARKETABLE SECURITIES	(Schedule 2)		787,638
NON-MARKETABLE SECURITIES	(Schedule 3)		0
INVESTMENTS IN PARTNERSHIPS	(Schedule 4)		0
REAL ESTATE (HOMESTEAD)	(Schedule 5)		170,000
REAL ESTATE (OTHER)	(Schedule 6)		6,577,220
IRA'S & RETIREMENT PLANS	(Schedule 7)		1,907,257
OIL & GAS INTERESTS	(Schedule 8)		
OTHER ASSETS			
Personal Property			10,000
Automobiles			30,000
Notes Receivable			
Interest in Trusts			
Misc.			
TOTAL ASSETS			**$9,883,774**

tent as well? As illustrated in Figure 5-3 and Figure 5-4, the answer to this question is that they are not the same. The REO Schedule on page 3 of the Fannie Mae Form 1003, as shown in Figure 5-3, is quite different from the REO Schedule of a generic fill-in-the-blank form, as illustrated in Figure 5-4.

Referring back to Figure 5-1, the parenthetical note in the real estate line instructs the loan applicant to enter the "total market value from the schedule of real estate owned," which is provided for on page 3 of the Fannie Mae 1003 loan application. This particular REO Schedule has enough space for three properties and provides about half of the number of columns that is required by most lenders. The REO Schedule shown in Figure 5-3 is essentially useless to a commercial real estate underwriter because it is inferior in so many ways. The primary problem is that the schedule lacks the correct number of rows and columns. Without a sufficient number of columns, critical information such as name of property, date of acquisition, original cost, percentage of ownership, name of the existing lender, and operating expenses will be excluded from the schedule. Another significant deficiency is the ill-defined column headings, such as the column heading labeled "Gross Rental Income." The problem with this heading is that it doesn't clearly communicate which type of gross rental income. Is the lender asking for monthly or annual gross rental income, and does "gross rental income" refer to income before vacancy loss or to "net rental income" after vacancy loss? Also, there's no column for total operating expenses. There are several more deficiencies, as well. The point about this type of REO Schedule, found on the Fannie Mae Form 1003 loan application, should be obvious.

The REO Schedule of a generic bank form, as illustrated in Figure 5-4, is not any better than the Fannie Mae version and likewise is deficient in many ways. You will recall that the asset section of the balance sheet,

Figure 5-3.REO Schedule Found on Page 3, Fannie Mae Form 1003.

VI. ASSETS AND LIABILITIES (cont.)							
Schedule of Real Estate Owned (If additional properties are owned, use continuation sheet.)							
Property Address (enter S if sold, PS if pending sale or R if rental being held for Income)	Type of Property	Present Market Value	Amount of Mortgages & Liens	Gross Rental Income	Mortgage Payments	Insurance Maintenance Taxes & Misc.	Net Rental Income
		$	$	$	$	$	$
	Totals	$ 0	$ 0	$ 0	$ 0	$ 0	$ 0

List any additional names under which credit has been previously received and indicate appropriate creditor name(s) and account number(s):

illustrated in Figure 5-2, includes a parenthetical note in the real estate line that instructs the loan applicant to enter the total market value as shown on Schedule 6. That schedule is shown in Figure 5-4.

Though Schedule 6 has the same number of columns as the Fannie Mae REO Schedule, the column headings are quite different. For example, a lender who receives a completed Fannie Mae REO Schedule will not know the original cost of the property or the percentage of ownership interest. Likewise, the same lender who receives a completed Schedule 6 will not have a description of the property nor will they know the net rental income. As we have noted, there is very little consistency among fill-in-the-blank type of REO Schedules, making it difficult for lenders to conduct their underwriting. Neither schedule is really adequate for commercial real estate. Because of the significant deficiencies, these schedules and others like them are not recommended for use. These schedules are just examples of the types of REO Schedules that are used every day by

Figure 5-4. REO Schedule of a Generic Bank Form.

SCHEDULE 6 – REAL ESTATE (OTHER)

LOCATION	PERCENT OWNED	COST	MARKET VALUE	DEBT	LIENHLDR	ANNUAL PAYMENTS	ANNUAL INCOME	ANNUAL EXPENSE
3101 Spencer Hwy. Pasadena T.	53.33%	5,559,190	6,577,220	4,783,675	Arbor Com M	319,800	1,119,300	684,372
			$ 6,577,220	$ 4,783,675	Arbor Com M	$ 319,800	$ 1,119,300	$ 684,372

borrowers and mortgage brokers. Though the Fannie Mae 1003 Form is really designed for residential lending, it is used quite often by mortgage brokers when applying for commercial loans. This form, like many other types of balance sheets that are available, has a very poorly designed REO Schedule. It is for this reason that commercial lenders and underwriters prefer the type of REO Schedule that is discussed in this chapter. In summary, instead of trying to embrace and comprehend all of the different types of REO Schedules, it's better to stick with one universal REO Schedule that can be used and attached to any balance sheet.

Anatomy of an REO Schedule

An REO Schedule is nothing more than a list of real estate assets, in rows and columns, formatted on a legal-size sheet of paper in a landscape orientation. The rows contain information concerning each property, and the columns contain information specific to each property. It is important to note that the standard eleven-inch length of a letter-size sheet of paper (in landscape orientation) is usually inadequate to accommodate the seventeen columns that are recommended and discussed in this chapter. In order to accommodate all of the seventeen columns on one page without reducing the font size beyond readability, it is better to expand the page width to fourteen inches (legal size). REO Schedules are usually created using a spreadsheet software program such as Microsoft Excel. If you are using Excel, we recommend that you set the font size for 11-point type with half-inch left and right margins. With a page scale of approximately 69 percent and the number of columns limited to seventeen (column A to column Q), you should be able to fit the schedule nicely on a legal-size sheet of paper.

The length of the schedule depends on the number of properties listed in the rows. One legal-size sheet in a landscape orientation can

usually accommodate approximately twelve properties. Overall, what
is important, more than formatting or anything else about the page
setup, is that you make sure to keep all seventeen column headings
on one page. Breaking up the column headings makes it much hard-
er for the lender to follow.

As illustrated in Figure 5-5, the REO Schedule comprises two
main sections, the *property value section* and the *cash flow section*. As
previously mentioned, the REO schedule is an extremely important
document to a commercial lender. Why? A seasoned commercial
lender can essentially sum up a borrower's ownership experience,
net worth, and free cash flow, all from just this one document.
However, without the right information, the REO schedule becomes
nothing more than a jigsaw puzzle with hundreds of missing pieces
that raises more questions than it answers.

Since an REO Schedule is prepared with a spreadsheet program
such as Excel or Lotus, it is best to describe the breakdown of both
the property value section and the cash flow section in terms of
columns and *rows*. The *property value section* is the larger of the two
sections and is composed of twelve columns; the number of rows is
dependent on the total number of properties. Some of the column
headings are self-explanatory, while others are not. The following column headings make up the entire property value section and are listed on the spreadsheet starting from left to right.

Property Value Section
- Name of Property
- Property Description
- Property Address
- Date of Acquisition
- Original Cost
- Name & Address of Lender
- Loan Number

Figure 5-5. Schedule of Real Estate Owned (REO Schedule).

Property Value Section

Name of Property	Property Description	Address	Date of Acquisition	Original Cost	Name & Address of Lender	Loan No.	(A) % Ownership
Woodway Square	Apartments 180 Units	900 West Rd Houston, TX	May-02	$5,000,000	Commerce Bank Houston, TX	50263	**50%**
Mountain View	Retail Center 20,000 SF	230 Hwy 80 Austin, TX	Jul-98	$2,500,000	First American Austin, TX	745055	**50%**
Rivercrest Professional	Office Building 50,000 SF	10001 Carey Rd Houston, TX	Feb-05	$4,000,000	Texas National Dallas, TX	100356	**100%**
Village Industrial Park	Warehouse 75,000 SF	100 Center St Spring, TX	Sep-08	$1,500,000	Sun Bank & Trust Houston, TX	600385	**25%**
Cedar Grove	Land 90 acres	12100 Hwy 144 Granbury, TX	Aug-07	$600,000	n/a	n/a	**100%**
Personal Residence	House 4,500 SF	5200 Gray St. Houston, TX	Jan-03	$400,000	Wells Fargo Houston, TX	1050009	**100%**
						TOTALS	

SOURCES OF INCOME

	Monthly	Annual
Salary (W-2 Wages)	$4,500	$54,000
Interest Income	$1,000	$12,000
Real Estate Investments	$24,000	$288,000
Other	$500	$6,000
Total Income	$30,000	$360,000

(continues)

Figure 5-5. (Continued.)

					Cash Flow Section				
Market Value	Balance of Mortgages (1st & 2nd Liens)	(B) Total Equity	(A) x (B) Net Ownership Equity	Monthly Rental Income	Monthly Operational Expenses	Monthly Loan Pymt.	(C) Monthly Cash Flow	(A) x (C) Net Ownership Cash Flow
$7,200,000	$5,000,000	$2,200,000	$1,100,000	$88,500	($46,541)	($33,959)	$8,000	$4,000
$3,000,000	$1,750,000	$1,250,000	$625,000	$25,000	($5,000)	($14,200)	$5,800	$2,900
$5,200,000	$2,750,000	$2,450,000	$2,450,000	$75,000	($37,500)	($17,800)	$19,700	$19,700
$3,000,000	$2,000,000	$1,000,000	$250,000	$38,000	($16,000)	($14,000)	$8,000	$2,000
$1,000,000	$25,000	$975,000	$975,000	$0	($1,500)	($100)	($1,600)	($1,600)
$600,000	$500,000	$100,000	$100,000	$0	$0	($3,000)	($3,000)	($3,000)
$20,000,000	$12,025,000	$7,975,000	**$5,500,000**	$226,500	($106,541)	($83,059)	$36,900	**$24,000**

- ➤ % Ownership
- ➤ Market Value
- ➤ Balance of Mortgages (1st & 2nd Liens)
- ➤ Total Equity
- ➤ Net Ownership Equity

The *cash flow section* is the smaller of the two sections and is composed of five columns; the number of rows is limited to the total number of properties. Three of the five columns are blank cells, which require a dollar value. The last two columns are formula cells that do not require any input of values and are automatically calculated on the basis of the values in the preceding columns. The following column headings make up the entire *cash flow section* and are listed on the spreadsheet following the Net Ownership Equity column, moving from left to right:

Cash Flow Section
- ➤ Monthly Rental Income
- ➤ Monthly Operational Expenses
- ➤ Monthly Loan Payment
- ➤ Monthly Cash Flow
- ➤ Net Ownership Cash Flow

Property Value Section

The property value section is used primarily to calculate the borrower's net worth or net equity in real estate. Note that the phrase "net worth in real estate" is used. Though a borrower may have a large net worth, as explained in Chapter 3, it's the net worth or net ownership equity in real estate that a commercial lender is most interested in. Since a borrower is presumed to be engaged in the commercial real estate business full time, it can be safe to assume that a borrower's net worth is mostly vested in real estate assets. A high net worth is good, but a high net worth in real estate is even better, and that's the reason that the property value section is extremely useful to the lender.

When attempting to complete the REO Schedule, it's usually a good idea to move from left to right across the table. The first few column headings are self-explanatory and can be completed quite easily. However, beginning with the Date of Acquisition column, the requested information becomes specific and detailed and may require a little research. Most likely, the borrower will not remember such detailed information and will need time to reference property files in order to correctly and accurately complete the schedule. The importance of being accurate cannot be stressed enough, and any attempt to fudge or guess at the information may result in the lender's rejection of the REO Schedule, causing further delay in processing the loan.

Property Name

Commercial properties are usually assigned project names such as Oak Tree Apartments or Highland Village Shopping Center. A *property name* is not a legal name for the property but merely a trade name or signature used by the owner. Property names are often omitted, making it difficult to differentiate one property from another. It's not absolutely necessary, but lenders like details, so be sure to include the property name or, if there is no official building name, make one up for easy reference. For example, if the property is an office building located on Jackson Street but doesn't have an official building name, make up a reference name like "Jackson Office Building." Sometimes a property is referenced by using the actual name of the partnership, such as Tree Top Apartments, LP.

Identifying properties in this way can be extremely helpful if the same name is displayed at the top of the property's P&L statement, helping the lender keep stacks of property P&L statements matched with the right property.

Property Description

The *property description* is important because it, first and foremost, tips off the lender as to whether the property is residential or commercial. For whatever reason, many borrowers fail time after time to provide a brief description of the property. At best, borrowers just put down an address, omitting the property's name and description. This column is usually only half an inch wide, so the description must be abbreviated. For example, an apartment complex can be abbreviated "APTS." For apartment buildings, since they can range in size from as few as 5 units to as many as 1,000, it's best to also include the number of units. Lenders like to see the number of units because it tells them that the borrower is capable of owning and perhaps managing large apartment complexes. Without the unit sizes, a lender may question the borrower's ownership strength. All other commercial properties are measured in size using square feet. If there is enough space or room in the field of this column, go ahead and try to include the number of net rentable square feet of the building, though it is not necessary.

Property Address

The *property address* should be a physical mailing address and one that can be mapped, unlike a post office box. A property address also tells a lender whether a borrower is diversified geographically or if the borrower is overweighted in a single market. If a borrower owns properties in several states, that means the borrower is capable of delegating or depending on other people to manage her properties.

On the other hand, the borrower may soon find herself losing money and control because of the difficulties of managing a property long distance. No matter where the properties are located, the addresses provide vital information about the borrower's ownership experience in various markets. The property address column should contain the entire physical address. If the street address is not known, at least provide the city and state.

Date of Acquisition

Lenders like to know how long a borrower has owned a property, and the only way for the lender to know that is to provide the *date of acquisition*. It's not necessary to provide the exact closing date, but at least try to provide the correct month and year. Putting down just the year may still raise questions if the date of acquisition was only last year. For example, if the borrower is trying to get a cash-out refinance, the lender will want to know if the borrower has owned the property for at least twelve months. If the current date is June 2009 but the date of acquisition of the property is shown only as 2008, without the month, the lender may question the length of ownership. If the purchase date was August 2008, then it's obvious the borrower has not owned the property long enough to satisfy the twelve-month requirement. So try to pin down the month and year. It will stave off one more question from the lender.

Original Cost of the Property

The *original cost* or the original purchase price tells the lender how much the property has appreciated since the acquisition date. Of course, the property may have been expanded or extensively renovated, adding additional value, but at least the lender will have some basis to work from when comparing the original price to the current market value. Be watchful for market values that are significantly higher than or even double the original purchase price. A borrower who purchased an apartment complex two years ago at a cost of $5 million but now is claiming its market value to be $10 million is an example that will and should raise a red flag with any lender. Unless the borrower spent an additional $2 million to $3 million in capital improvements, it is highly doubtful that the value could have doubled in two years. If the property was purchased more than five years ago, the cost becomes less relevant to the lender because of the length of time. So the rule of thumb is that if the date of acquisition is less than five years ago, be sure to hunt down that original cost. If it is missing, the lender will eventually ask for it at some point.

Name and Address of Lender

If a property listed on an REO Schedule is currently encumbered with a mortgage, it is very important to include both the *name and address of the lender* that currently holds the first lien to the property. It is sometimes necessary to include the name and address of the second lien holder if one exists, as well. Providing the name of each lender is akin to dropping names at a party, especially if you are trying to make a good first impression. Borrowers that have successfully borrowed from large national banks with household names like Citibank, Wells Fargo, or Bank of America are viewed as extremely creditworthy. So be sure to provide the names of all lenders and the city where the existing loan with each lender was originated.

Loan Number

The *loan number* is not really necessary, but this column is found on most REO Schedules, so it is worth mentioning here. The purpose of the loan number is to aid the new lender in verifying the history of mortgage payments with the existing lender at a later time. But usu-

ally there is a separate document that the new lender uses to under-
take that task. If the borrower has the loan number readily available,
it's best to put on the schedule now rather than later.

Ownership Percentage

The *ownership percentage* column is designed to input the borrower's
ownership interest in the property in percentage points. For example,
if a borrower has only one partner, the borrower must indicate what
percentage of the property he owns. Is it 50 percent, 20 percent, or 5
percent? If title to the property is vested in a corporation, a limited liability company, or a limited partnership, the borrower must indicate
his percentage ownership interest in the partnership or company.
Ownership interest and capital contribution can be two different percentages, but it is the ownership interest that the lender is most interested in. This ownership percentage is usually stated in the partnership
agreement. There must be written evidence in the form of documentation proving a borrower's percentage of ownership interest. The percentage of a borrower's ownership interest can also be found in the
partnership tax returns (IRS Form 1065, Schedule K-1) or in partnership agreements, operating agreements, or tenancy-in-common agreements, which are all acceptable forms of documentation.

Market Value of the Property

Market value is intended to represent the current value of the property if sold on the open market. This is the place on the REO
Schedule where most borrowers tend to embellish a little, if not a lot.
The lender will not assume that the values shown in this column of
the REO Schedule are bona fide market values. Market value is
intended to be the property's current "as-is" value. There must be

some basis for these values; the borrower cannot just pull them out of the air. There are three principal sources that are generally accepted by all lenders in determining a property's current "as-is" market value. These three sources for deriving the market value are:

- ➤ Settlement or closing statement
- ➤ Appraisal
- ➤ Profit-and-loss statement ✓

The first and preferred source is the borrower's *original settlement* or *closing statement*. The original settlement or closing statement discloses the original sales price, stifling any argument regarding the market value. Of course if the property was purchased several years ago, this method does not account for any capital appreciation. So it depends how long the borrower has owned the property. The rule of thumb is that if the property was purchased less than two years ago, it's best to use the original sales price as provided on the original settlement statement. If the borrower incurred any additional costs for any significant capital improvements then these costs should be added to the original purchase price.

The second source that can be used as the basis for the property's market value is an *appraisal* prepared by an MAI. MAI is the acronym for Member of the Appraisal Institute, which is the highest designation for a real estate appraiser. It's not a state license but an industry certification, one that is extremely difficult to attain. If the borrower has had the property appraised within the past year, that value can be used. However, there are many types of valuations. For example, there can be a "stabilized as-completed value" or a "stabilized as-repaired value," just to name two, but the only appraised value acceptable to a lender is the "as-is" value and nothing else. It also depends on who ordered the appraisal or for whom the appraisal was prepared. If the borrower ordered the appraisal, a lender may be suspicious of the value because the appraiser may have been influenced by the borrower. An appraiser engaged by a previous lender who was instructed to perform an appraisal per the lender's instructions is much more credible and more likely to be seen as an acceptable source for estimating the property's current market value. Lenders structure loans primarily on the basis of current "as-is" values and not on future values, as the phrase "stabilized value" implies. "As-is" value refers to the market value of the property in its current physical condition and current occupancy without any consideration of future renovations or repairs. "Stabilized value" is the maximum market value attainable based on the assumption that property has reached its optimum performance and occupancy within its sub-market. The phrases "as-completed" and "as-repaired" added to the word "stabilized" suggest that either the property is currently under construction or that it is currently being repaired. Therefore, the phrases "stabilized as-completed" and "as-repaired" simply mean the maximum market value upon the completion of the construction and the maximum market value upon the completion of the repairs, respectively.

The third source for deriving a property's market value, which is often used by lenders if neither of the other sources is available, is the *property's profit-and-loss statement* (P&Ls). The profit-and-loss statement must cover either a full calendar year or be a trailing twelve-month statement of income and all operational expenses. The resulting net operating income, or NOI, is then capitalized to derive the property's current market value. For example, if the profit-and-loss statement indicates that the NOI is $100,000, the property will be valued by dividing $100,000 by 10 percent (0.10), resulting in a $1,000,000 capitalized value. This method, of course, involves guessing at what the capitalization rate should be and can result in either an understated or overstated market value. Nevertheless, if the borrower has owned the property more than two years and doesn't want to use the original sales price and there is no recent appraisal, then it is best to capitalize the NOI using the profit-and-loss statement. In fact, many lenders use this method even if there is an appraisal or a closing statement showing the original sales price as a way of testing the current cash flow against these proven values. For example, if there has been an increase in operating expenses or income and occupancy is on the decline since the effective date of the most recent appraisal, it is safe to assume that the property value is in decline as well, thus making this method a safeguard for the lender.

Balance of Mortgages

An REO Schedule must include the *balance of mortgages* for each property encumbered by a first lien. What the lender is after here is the borrower's current total debt on the property, which should include all subordinate liens. Often the amount of the new loan request is insufficient to pay off all of the existing loans, so it is very important to make sure that the total balance shown in this column truly represents the total outstanding balance of all liens. Many times borrowers omit the second or even third liens, creating confusion for the new lender. First liens, second liens, and even third liens must be added to show how much debt is owed against the property. This amount can help the lender determine the *loan-to-value* (LTV) ratios for each property. For example, if the market value is stated to be $5 million and the total debt is $4.5 million, then the borrower's current LTV on this property is 90 percent. That is a highly leveraged property, which lenders consider unacceptable. However, if the aggregate market value for all of the properties is $20 million and the aggregate debt is $15 million, then the aggregate LTV is much lower at 75 percent. A lender can tolerate a few properties that may be over-leveraged as long as the aggregate leverage is in line with the usual

LTV maximum level of 75 percent. Be sure to confirm these debt amounts; after all, it is not a good idea to keep the lender guessing, only to have the lender find out later that the debts were much higher than disclosed. Keep in mind that personal credit reports do not disclose past or current commercial loans, so there is no way for a lender to verify these amounts without a loan number and the name of the lender.

Total Equity

Total equity represents the residual ownership interest in the market value of the property remaining after subtracting all of the property's debts. Total equity is another way of describing an owner's net worth in a given property. The cell or field in this column of the spreadsheet is automatically calculated using values located in the "market value" column and in the "balance of mortgages" column. Total equity is derived by subtracting outstanding mortgages from the property's market value.

Market Value − Balance of Mortgages = Total Equity

$5,000,000 − $2,000,000 = $3,000,000

Total equity, sometimes referred to as "market equity," as defined in Chapter 3, is usually a combination of cash, referred to as "cash equity" (the original down payment) and value appreciation. If the property was purchased less than a year ago, then total equity will consist of only cash equity (the original down payment). The operative word in the phrase market equity is "market," which simply means that total equity is derived using the property's market value and not its original cost. Depending on how long the borrower has owned the property, there may not be any cash equity left in the property, meaning that the borrower has pulled out his original cash equity some time ago when the property was refinanced. If the property was recently purchased, most likely the market equity is the borrower's original cash down payment. There can be many analytical interpretations resulting from these figures, but what is important is to be as accurate and precise as possible when presenting both the market value figure and the property's existing debt. Remember, it's the lender's job to make sense of what constitutes cash equity or value appreciation.

Net Ownership Equity

The last column in the property value section is the *net ownership equity* column, which shows the borrower's pro rata share of the total equity shown in terms of a dollar amount. "Pro rata share" refers to a borrower's portion of the total equity expressed in percentage points (e.g., 10%, 50%). This column is a value cell that automatically calculates the borrower's share of the total equity shown in the preceding column. This particular field or cell on the REO Schedule is designed for borrowers who are joint property owners and cannot claim 100 percent of the total equity in the property. The formula in this cell is simply the "ownership percentage (%)" multiplied by the "total equity," resulting in the borrower's net ownership equity or pro rata share of the property's total equity. For example, a borrower with a 50 percent ownership interest can claim 50 percent of the total property equity. If total property equity is $3,000,000, the borrower's pro rata share of the total equity or net ownership equity is only $1,500,000.

$$\text{Ownership Percentage} \times \text{Total Equity} = \text{Net Ownership Equity}$$

$$0.50 \times \$3,000,000 = \$1,500,000$$

There's no official terminology for describing "net ownership equi-ty," so it is not unusual to hear alternative phrases such as the "bor-rower's pro rata share of equity," "borrower's net equity," or "net worth in real estate." What is of the utmost importance is that this column accurately represent only that percentage of the total equity of which the borrower can claim ownership. The summation of these different ownership percentages of the total equity is calculated at the bottom of this column and represents the borrower's aggregate pro rata share of the entire portfolio's total equity in real estate. Aside from other assets, such as cash and marketable securities, which may be offset by additional liabilities, this aggregate pro rata share of the total equity in real estate is what a borrower's true net worth is to a lender. Of course, there may be other assets that account for 10 to 30 percent of a borrower's overall net worth, but it's the net worth in real estate that is of the greatest interest to a lender.

Cash Flow Section

The *cash flow section* is used primarily to calculate the borrower's pro rata share of the property's net cash flow, as discussed in Chapter 3. In order to accurately complete this section of the REO Schedule, the borrower will need a full year-end profit-and-loss statement or a trail-ing twelve-month profit-and-loss statement.

It's usually not a good idea to use a year-to-date P&L statement because it does not represent a full twelve months and because many expenses, such as real estate taxes and utility reimbursements, are not accounted for until the end of the year or the beginning of the next year. The omission of certain operating expenses or even income resulting from a cash accounting method may result in an overstatement or an understatement of NOI. Often year-to-date P&L statements are annualized to simulate a full year-end P&L statement. Annualizing is a method that involves calculating the average monthly NOI based on the year-to-date number of months and then multiplying that average monthly figure by twelve months. For example, if the P&L statement is a year-to-date statement ending July 31, the total NOI for the first seven months is divided by seven to derive the monthly average over the last seven months. This monthly average figure is then multiplied by twelve to arrive at the annualized figure. Again, this is not recommended and can result in a skewed or erroneous NOI for the property. It's best to use the most recent full year-end P&L statement or at least a trailing twelve-month statement.

Monthly Rental Income

The first column in the cash flow section of the REO Schedule begins by asking for the property's *monthly rental income.* Monthly rental income may at first appear to be self-explanatory, but there is really only one figure considered suitable for this column. You may ask, "What is so complicated or difficult about filling in this column on the REO Schedule?" Well, if you have any experience analyzing or reviewing profit-and-loss statements, you will agree that there is often more than one category of income. Therefore, choosing the right category becomes the challenge. As illustrated in Figure 5-6, there are five major income categories included in the income section of a typical P&L statement.

These five major income categories are identified with an asterisk; they are gross potential income, gross rental income, net rental income, total other income, and effective gross income. The sample P&L statement presented in Figure 5-6 is a monthly statement for the month of December and includes both a "current month column" and a "year-to-date column." However, P&L statements never include a column for monthly averages. This column which was added to Figure 5-6, is merely a visual aid for reference. Since the P&L statement is a December statement, it provides both the current total

Figure 5-6. Income Section of a P&L Statement.

INCOME	Current Month (December)	Year-to-Date (Jan.–Dec.)	Monthly Average
Gross Potential Income*	$100,000	$1,200,000	$100,000
Loss-to-Lease	($5,000)	($97,000)	($8,083)
Gross Rental Income*	$95,000	$1,103,000	$91,917
LESS:			
Concessions	($3,500)	($63,000)	($5,250)
Bad Debt & Collection Loss	($1,500)	($23,000)	($1,917)
Vacancy	($7,500)	($83,000)	($6,917)
Net Rental Income*	$82,500	$934,000	$77,833
Other Income			
Laundry and Vending	$750	$8,400	$700
Application Fees	$450	$4,700	$392
NSF and Late Fees	$275	$2,700	$225
Parking Income	$950	$13,500	$1,125
Water Reimbursements	$2,500	$27,500	$2,292
Forfeited Security Deposits	$1,075	$8,700	$725
Total Other Income*	$6,000	$65,500	$5,459
Effective Gross Income* (EGI)	$88,500	$999,500	$83,292

monthly figures and the twelve-month total for the months January through December. This particular P&L statement is what is referred to as a December year-end P&L statement in which the year-to-date column accounts for all twelve months of the year. If the P&L statement is for the current month of August, the year-to-date column will include the eight-month total of income for the months January through August.

Now that the distinction between the rental income categories and the current month and year-to-date columns has been illustrated, it's time to choose the appropriate monthly rental income figure, which is the first value in the cash flow section. As shown in the sample income section of the P&L statement, there are many sources and categories of income. The question now is which category of income should be the one used to represent the monthly rental income. The answer is *effective gross income*, also referred to its widely known abbreviation, *EGI*. As illustrated in Figure 5-6, effective gross income represents a property's total monthly revenue after factoring in vacancy, bad debts, concessions, and other income. Using any other income category may result in either an overstatement or understatement of the property's monthly rental income, which is why it's best to always use the effective gross income shown on the P&L statement. It is a misrepresentation of facts if one carelessly throws in a total rental income figure without accounting for loss-to-lease, concessions, bad debts, vacancy, and other income.

The effective gross income for the month of December in Figure 5-6 is $88,500, but you will also notice that there is a column indicating a monthly average of $83,292. In this example, the correct value to use in the monthly rental income column of the cash flow section is $88,500, primarily because it is simply higher than the monthly average. However, before moving on to the operational expenses, it is important to note that the annual or year-to-date total effective gross income is $999,500. If this figure is divided by twelve months, the resulting monthly average is $83,292. In this situation, the current month is higher than the twelve-month average and thus is the appropriate value to use. Sometimes the monthly average is actually higher than the current month because of a sudden drop in occupancy. In that situation, it is best to use the monthly average instead of the current month.

Monthly Operating Expenses

The second column in the cash flow section of the REO Schedule is where *monthly operating expenses* should be entered. As pointed out in the monthly rental income section, either the full year-end P&L statement or a trailing twelve-month P&L statement should be used in calculating monthly operating expenses. Unlike a current monthly statement of income, which reflects the property's actual rental income for the current month and presumably the monthly rental income going forward, operating expenses are seasonal and vary significantly from month to month. In the monthly rental income section, we suggest that the greater of either the current month's effective gross income or a monthly average of the year-to-date total could be used. However, a current month's total operating expenses may be skewed due to seasonally high utility costs or nonrecurring legal expenses related to an eviction, for example. It is for this reason that monthly P&L statements should never be used. Figure 5-7 illustrates a typical operating expense section of a December P&L statement, reflecting the current month's operating expenses with a year-to-date column and a monthly average column.

As illustrated in Figure 5-7, total operating expenses for the current month of December are $36,021. December's monthly operating expense is $10,520 lower than the monthly average of $46,541, which was derived from the total year-to-date operating expense of $558,500 divided by twelve. Using the December monthly expense of $36,021 would grossly understate the property's operating expenses by $10,520 per month and by an annual amount of $126,240. Therefore, it is recommended that a monthly average be used, which will smooth out the highs and lows during the twelve-month period. Always take the total annual operating expense either from the year-end statement or a trailing twelve-month statement and then divide that total annual figure by twelve to arrive at this monthly average.

Before trying to calculate the monthly average, remember this point: most operating expense sections of P&L statements include nonoperating expenses such as mortgage interest, asset/partnership fees, amortization, and depreciation, as illustrated in Figure 5-7.

Figure 5-7. Operating Expense Section of a P&L Statement.

OPERATING EXPENSES	Current Month (December)	Year-to-Date (Jan.–Dec.	Monthly Average
Real Estate Taxes	$5,000	$145,000	$12,083
Insurance	$1,785	$40,000	$3,333
~~Mortgage Interest~~	~~$0~~	~~$540,000~~	~~$0~~
Utilities	$8,560	$45,000	$3,750
Repairs and Maintenance	$1,800	$65,000	$5,417
Cleaning and Make Ready	$1,269	$20,000	$1,667
Supplies	$879	$15,000	$1,250
Grounds and Landscaping	$900	$14,000	$1,167
Pest Control	$35	$1,800	$150
Pool	$120	$6,800	$567
Salaries	$8,880	$120,000	$10,000
~~Asset/Partnership Mgmt Fee~~	~~$0~~	~~$20,000~~	~~$0~~
Telephone	$175	$2,500	$208
Management Fee	$3,333	$40,000	$3,333
~~Amortization~~	~~$0~~	~~$7,000~~	~~$0~~
General and Administrative	$575	$10,000	$833
Marketing and Leasing	$435	$15,000	$1,250
~~Depreciation~~	~~$0~~	~~$250,000~~	~~$0~~
Miscellaneous	$275	$6,400	$533
Legal and Professional Fees	$2,000	$12,000	$1,000
Total Operating Expenses	$36,021	$558,500	$46,541

These nonoperating expenses should always be excluded when calculating both monthly and annual operating expenses. If not, the
monthly average will be grossly overstated by as much as $68,083
per month or by as much as $817,000 annually. Therefore, be on the
lookout for these types of nonoperating expenses, and be sure to
exclude them when calculating the monthly average.

Monthly Loan Payments

The *monthly loan payment* column is fairly straightforward, with only
a few minor exceptions. The cells in this column, like those in the
monthly rental income and monthly operating expense columns, are
intentionally left blank, requiring the borrower or mortgage broker to
enter a value. The monthly loan payment should include both principal and interest if the loan is amortizing. However, the figure
should not include any monthly escrows such as real estate taxes,
insurance, or capital replacement reserves. These were already
included in the monthly operating expenses previously discussed. Be
sure to add to the first lien payment all other second and third lien
monthly payments, as well. Sometimes the monthly loan payment
on a loan for the property listed on the REO Schedule covers interest
only. Most interest-only loan payments are short-term, usually less
than two years, depending on the type of loan. It is perfectly fine to
use the monthly interest-only payment if the loan has no amortizing
component, meaning that it is probably a short term loan with
a balloon payment. However, if the interest-only monthly loan payment is temporary, with amortization kicking in after a year, it is
better to use the principal and interest payment instead of the
interest-only payment. Using the interest-only payment, which will
eventually convert to an amortizing payment of principal and interest, can grossly overstate the property's monthly net cash flow. Look
for these aberrations like short-term interest-only payments when

calculating a property's monthly net cash flow, and instead try using monthly debt service payments that are amortizing.

Monthly Cash Flow

Monthly cash flow within the cash flow section of the REO Schedule represents the property's monthly cash flow after debt service. It is important to emphasize the phrase "after debt service"; this should not be confused with a similar cash flow term called NOI (net operating income). NOI is a property's cash flow before debt service. The cell or field in this column of the spreadsheet is automatically calculated using values taken from the monthly rental income column, the monthly operating expenses column, and the monthly loan payments column. Monthly cash flow is derived by subtracting monthly operating expenses and monthly loan payments from monthly rental income. For example, using the values presented in Figure 5-6 and Figure 5-7 and adding a monthly loan payment of $33,959 results in a monthly cash flow of $8,000:

$$\begin{array}{c} \text{Monthly} \\ \text{Rental Income} \end{array} - \begin{array}{c} \text{Monthly} \\ \text{Operating Expenses} \end{array} - \begin{array}{c} \text{Monthly} \\ \text{Loan Payments} \end{array} = \begin{array}{c} \text{Monthly Cash Flow} \end{array}$$

$$\$88,500 - \$46,541 - \$33,959 = \$8,000$$

The property's monthly cash flow in this column is commonly referred to as *cash flow after debt service* (CFADS) or *net cash flow,* as described in Chapter 3. Monthly cash flow, shown here, represents 100 percent of the income that is passed through to the owners of the property. If the property has only one owner, presumably the borrower, then 100 percent of this monthly cash flow can be claimed by the borrower. If there are partners who can claim a portion of that cash flow, then only the borrower's percentage is relevant to the lender. The next column in the cash flow section of the REO Schedule deals exactly with that issue of fractured ownership and is discussed next.

Net Ownership Cash Flow

The final column within the cash flow section of the REO Schedule is the borrower's *net ownership cash flow*. There is nothing to enter into this column. It is a value cell containing a formula that automatically calculates the borrower's share of the total monthly cash flow, which was automatically calculated in the preceding column. As illustrated in Figure 5-5, the owner of Woodway Square Apartments is not the sole owner. He cannot claim 100 percent of the monthly cash flow, just as he cannot claim 100 percent of the total equity in the property. Net ownership cash flow is calculated by multiplying monthly cash flow by the percentage of ownership interest indicated in the property value section. The product of this calculation represents the borrower's pro rata share of the property's total monthly cash flow:

Monthly Cash Flow × % Ownership = Net Ownership Cash Flow

$8,000 × 0.50 = $4,000

As demonstrated in the previous example, the total monthly cash flow generated by the property's operations is $8,000. Since the borrower owns only 50 percent of the asset, only 50 percent of the cash flow can be claimed by the borrower. If the borrower owns more than one property, these individually calculated cash flows are summed at the bottom of the column. The total net ownership cash flow for all properties represents the borrower's aggregate pro rata share of the entire portfolio's cash flow, which is also referred to as the borrower's *aggregate net cash flow*, from real estate income as previously discussed in Chapter 3. This aggregated net cash flow derived from the borrower's investments in real estate is extremely important in that it helps the lender determine whether the portfolio's cash flow represents a significant portion of the borrower's total annual income. A borrower may have several sources of income, such as a salary, interest income, or stock dividends, but what is paramount to a lender is how much of that total annual income is derived from real estate, and that's why the cash flow section of the REO Schedule is extremely useful.

CHAPTER 6

FORMS OF OWNERSHIP

Every now and then, you may hear a lender, an attorney, or title company use the word *vested* in describing ownership of a property. Another popular phrase often used by title companies that refers to the ownership of a property is *owner of record*. Title to the property may be held in the name of an individual, a husband and wife, a corporation, or a trust. These are just a few of the many different types of *forms of ownership*. Why does this matter, and is there one form of ownership more advantageous than another? The answer depends squarely on one's corporate structure and tolerance for risk. Forms of ownership are generally classified as either an *individual* or a *legal entity*. In the commercial real estate lending industry, lenders and bankers often refer to individuals as *borrowers* and legal entities as *borrowing entities*. In this chapter we discuss the distinction between borrowers and borrowing entities and describe the different forms of ownership, such as tenants in common, partnerships, limited partnerships, limited liability companies, corporations, and trusts, along with their advantages and disadvantages.

Borrowers and Borrowing Entities

The words "borrower" and "borrowing entity" are distinctly different. The word "borrower" commonly refers to a person or individual, such as a single man, unmarried woman, or husband and wife. However, for commercial mortgages, the word "borrower" is often used broadly to refer to either an individual or a borrowing entity without regard to semantics. The broad use of the word "borrower" by commercial real estate lenders is really a matter of simplification on the part of loan officers, even though they know that the distinction between the two words can profoundly impact the structure and terms of the loan.

A borrower can consist of one or more individuals. Two or more individuals create multiple borrowers, who are commonly referred to as co-borrowers. Examples of co-borrowers include a husband and wife or two people working together as business partners. Individual borrowers and co-borrowers alike are always fully responsible for the full repayment of the loan. In other words, a co-borrower is equally responsible for the full repayment of the entire loan even if the other co-borrower becomes incapacitated for any reason. When the ownership of a property is shared by two individuals, it is often assumed that they share the debt, as well. This assumption is incorrect. Even though each co-owner owns 50 percent of the property, each remains individually liable for 100 percent of the loan at all times in spite of the divided ownership interests. This is what it means when lenders say that co-borrowers are *jointly* and *severally* liable for the full and unconditional repayment of the loan. Whether the borrower is composed of a single individual or multiple individuals, a lender will always assume that the borrower is a natural person unless the loan request in fact is made by a distinct legal or borrowing entity.

Generally speaking, the phrase "borrowing entity" is synonymous with the words "legal entity" and is distinct from the word "borrower" only in the sense that a borrowing entity is not a natural person or individual. The phrase "borrowing entity" is uniquely used by lenders so that it is clear to everyone that the borrower is a legal entity and not a natural person. Without getting too bogged down in legal definitions, a legal entity is an artificial organization created by state law that gives a person or group of persons a separate and distinct legal identity such as a corporation, trust, or limited partnership. A borrowing entity (legal entity) such as a corporation can own property, make contracts, and sue or be sued in its own name, thus insulating and protecting the owner or shareholders from personal liability. Because legal entities provide various legal protections from liabilities and lawsuits, individuals often form corporations or limited partnerships by which to protect themselves. Since a legal entity can purchase properties, these entities will inevitably need a loan. The name of the borrowing entity will always be the same as the name of the legal entity shown in the deed, which leads us right back to the question of how title to the property is vested. That question can easily be answered by conducting a title search. If the loan is for a refinance, a title search by the title company will disclose the current owner of record, which is assumed to be the borrowing entity as well. Unless the owner of record intends to transfer deed to a newly formed legal entity for tax or liability reasons, the lender will just assume that the name of the borrowing entity will be no different from the owner of record evidenced by the title report. However, a title search regarding a purchase loan is not necessary because the current owner of record will be the seller and not the buyer. A buyer involved in a purchase loan usually creates or forms a new legal entity and then later informs the lender of the new name. Exceptions to the creation of a new legal entity with regard to a purchase loan involves 1031 tax exchanges. IRS 1031 tax exchange rules limit exchanges to like properties and to like entities, meaning that the legal entity that sold the relinquished property must also be the same entity that purchases the replacement property.

Unlike a simple individual borrower that is nothing more than one person or persons, a borrowing entity can be a very complex ownership structure and can include multiple shell entities just within one corporation or limited partnership. For example, a limited partnership can have another limited partnership or a corporation named as its general partner, with many more limited partnerships as the limited partners. Usually it's the borrower's responsibility or that of the borrower's attorney to provide an organizational chart that looks like a corporate organizational flow chart. The organizational chart helps a lender understand who the key principals and managing members will be, along with their respective ownership interests. Many legal entities are relatively simple partnerships that involve only a general partner or managing member and a few limited partners, but others can be very convoluted, with dozens of individual and corporate limited partners, making it very difficult to identify the key principal capable of guaranteeing the loan. What is important to note here is that a lender needs to know who is in charge of managing the borrowing entity, including those individuals who might be needed to personally guarantee the loan. The organizational chart is the first place to start, and if it is still not clear how the borrowing entity is structured or who the key principals are, then it is best to do some further investigating before going any further with the loan.

Types of Borrowers and Borrowing Entities

There are many types of borrowers and borrowing entities in which title to the property can be vested. Often lenders ask, "How is title vested?" The word "vested" describes the lawful or legal owner shown on the title or deed to the property. In many instances, the name of the lawful owner shown on the deed or title will be the same as the name of the borrower or borrowing entity, although in purchase transactions the name of the legal entity has not yet been formed. However, it's not enough just to know the name of the borrower or borrowing entity; it is also very important to know the type of borrower or borrowing entity that will be responsible for paying back the loan. Since the borrower or borrowing entity is the same person or legal entity that owns or will own the commercial property, it stands to reason that a lender will also need to know the type of ownership. Each type or form of ownership presents its own set of problems and complications for the lender, so a basic understanding of the different forms of ownership can be very useful to investors, mortgage brokers, and borrowers alike. For a lender, the type or form of ownership can significantly affect the language and terms of the loan covenants and other loan documents, such as the deed of trust and guarantee agreement.

There are six general categories of ownership, with two of the six further divided into three separate and distinct forms of ownership commonly recognized by all commercial real estate lenders. These unique forms of ownership, which are discussed in the remainder of this chapter, include the following:

1. Individual ownership
2. Co-tenancy and joint ownership
   Tenancy in common

    Joint tenancy

    Tenancy by the entirety

  3. Partnerships

    General partnerships

    Limited partnerships

  4. Limited liability companies

  5. Corporations

  6. Trusts

Individual Ownership

Individual ownership involves no more than a single person and is the simplest and easiest to understand. As previously discussed, this type of ownership involves a natural person, not a legal entity, making the individual and the borrower one and the same. Often individual ownership involves a husband and wife, although each is considered by the lender an individual borrower or co-borrower. Technically speaking, an individual type of ownership is really the only appropriate situation where it is correct to refer to the individual as the borrower. As previously discussed, the word "borrower" can also be used loosely to refer to a borrowing entity, which is not an individual. It's really a matter of semantics, but it is always good to know the difference when talking with a lender.

   Though it may seem as though there is not much more to discuss concerning individual ownership, it is worth mentioning that there are thirteen different variations of individual ownership. These are necessary mainly because homestead and community property laws differ from state to state. It is up to the individual to decide how he is going to vest title to the property and not necessarily the lender. The lender is concerned only with selecting and preparing the correct set of loan documents for that type of individual ownership. For example, if an individual man is married but is going to put only his name on the title and not his wife's, the lender will refer to the borrower as a "married man as his sole and separate property." Or, if the man is divorced and is the only person to be named on the title, the lender must refer to the borrower as an "unmarried man." What is interesting is that this divorced man cannot be referred to as a "single man" because he has been married once already. If a man has never been married, he is referred to as a "single man." All of these technical differences have to do with state homestead, marriage, and community property laws. It is not necessary, nor is it within the scope of this chapter, to discuss the legal differences among the types of individual or husband-and-wife ownership. However, because of the complications caused by homestead and community property laws, it is extremely important that any individual consult an attorney before deciding on the type of individual ownership that will hold title to the property. These are the thirteen different types of individual ownership for a single individual or a husband and wife that are commonly used:

- ➤ Single man
- ➤ Unmarried man
- ➤ Single woman
- ➤ Unmarried woman
- ➤ Husband and wife
- ➤ Husband and wife as joint tenants
- ➤ Husband and wife as community property
- ➤ Husband and wife as tenants in common
- ➤ Widow/widower
- ➤ Tenants by the entirety
- ➤ Married man as his sole and separate property
- ➤ Married woman as her sole and separate property
- ➤ Husband and wife as joint tenants with rights of survivorship

Co-Tenancy and Joint Ownership

Co-tenancy is a form of ownership that involves more than one person. It has become a popular form of ownership for commercial investors just in the past ten years. Technically, a property owned by more than one person creates a concurrent estate or co-tenancy type of ownership. Co-tenancy is a concept in property law that describes the various ways in which property can be owned by more than one person at the same time. Two or more individuals or persons that own the same property are most commonly referred to as *co-owners, co-tenants,* or *joint tenants.* Three types of concurrent estate or co-tenancies are recognized by most states: *tenancy in common, joint tenancy,* and *tenancy by the entirety.* Each of these comes with its own unique set of rights regarding the co-tenants' or co-owners' right to use, possess, sell, encumber, devise, or sever their joint ownership of the property. This unique set of legal rights and obligations, along with their advantages and disadvantages, is a legal discussion best left to a real estate attorney and is not covered in this chapter.

Tenancy in Common

Tenancy in common is the most common type of joint ownership in which each owner, referred to as a tenant in common, is regarded by the law as owning separate and distinct shares of the same property. This form of ownership is most common where the co-owners are not married or have contributed different amounts to the acquisition of the property. Most states recognize tenancy in common in which there is no right of survivorship, meaning that, upon the death of one tenant in common, his or her ownership interest passes to his or her heirs (wife, children, relatives) as part of the estate. In other words, the other surviving co-tenant does not have any right or claim to the deceased co-tenant's interest in the property.

Tenancy in common has become such a popular and frequently

used form of ownership that its acronym, TIC, has become a household word among investors, real estate brokers, and those in the mortgage industry. Tenancies in common, or TICs (pronounced ticks), are frequently used in conjunction with 1031 tax exchanges. A 1031 tax exchange event occurs when a property owner sells her property for a gain and then replaces that same property by purchasing a similar property at a price equal to or greater than the sales price of the property that was sold in order to defer the tax on the capital gain. Since the IRS ruled that tenancies in common were eligible entities for 1031 tax exchanges, the number of TICs has quadrupled. As previously mentioned, tenancies in common allow more than one person to own the same property. What is unique and interesting about TICs is that each co-owner or co-tenant does not have to be a natural person. Unlike joint tenants, co-tenants or co-owners within a TIC can be legal entities such corporations, limited partnerships, or limited liability companies, which is why they are so popular for 1031 tax exchanges. Essentially, a TIC can be composed of two, three, or even ten co-tenants that are all limited liability companies. Whether the co-tenants are individuals or legal entities or a combination of these, there must be a written document called a *tenancy in common agreement* that identifies the controlling co-tenant and identifies all of the co-tenants, along with their respective ownership interests and capital contributions, among other things.

Joint Tenancy

Joint tenancy is another type of co-tenancy that is a form of ownership common among a husband and wife. However, there is no requirement that joint tenants be married or that there be only two joint tenants. Each individual owner in joint tenancy has a right to sell, encumber, and possess the entire property. What sets joint tenancy ownership apart from a tenancy in common is the right of survivor-

ship. In nearly every state, with the exception of a few states like
Texas, joint tenancy affords each joint tenant the right of survivorship, meaning that the ownership interest of the deceased joint tenant is passed on immediately to the surviving joint tenant. Unlike
many states, Texas does not allow joint tenants to automatically enjoy
a right of survivorship. Under Texas law, if one joint tenant dies
before the tenancy is severed, the interest owned by the deceased
joint tenant does not survive to the remaining joint tenants but
instead passes by will or intestacy. Overall, joint tenancy is not that
common among commercial property owners and is rarely encountered by commercial real estate lenders.

Tenancy by the Entirety

Tenancy by the entirety is a type of co-tenancy that was formerly available only to married couples. In it, ownership of property is treated
as though the couple were a single legal person. Like a joint tenancy,
a tenancy by the entirety also encompasses a right of survivorship, so
if one spouse dies, the entire interest in the property passes to the
surviving spouse without going through probate. Also, besides shar-
ing the four unities necessary to create a joint tenancy with right of
survivorship, which are time, title, interest, and possession, there
must also be the fifth unity of marriage. However, unlike a joint tenancy with right of survivorship, neither party in a tenancy by the
entirety has a unilateral right to sever the tenancy. Today, tenancy by
the entirety is rarely used as a form of ownership, and, in fact, many
states no longer recognize it.

Lenders' Treatment of Co-tenancy Ownership

A lender's view of a co-tenancy type of ownership is no different from
its view of an individual owner or a single borrower. As explained earlier in the description of tenancy in common, such arrangements

involve at least two or more co-owners, whether the owner is a natural person or a legal entity such as a corporation or limited liability company. To a lender, each of these co-owners is also a co-borrower, making each of them severally and jointly liable for the repayment of the loan. For example, if all but one of the co-tenants dies, the remaining sole surviving co-tenant will be responsible for full repayment of the entire loan amount. Even if a co-tenant hasn't died but fails to abide by the loan covenants or defaults on his portion of the loan, the other co-tenants are still ultimately responsible for this co-tenant's or any other co-tenant's share of all indebtedness. It is for this reason that every co-tenant is treated as a co-borrower and fully underwritten by analyzing his credit report and verifying assets, employment, and mortgage history. Many times co-tenants have bad credit or insufficient net worth or liquidity and would as individuals be rejected by the lender. However, if the sole personal guarantee of at least one co-tenant is strong enough, there is a reasonable chance that the lender will approve the loan, even if the financial contribution of another co-tenant is weak. If two out of five co-tenants have really bad credit, that may jeopardize the entire loan approval. These possible scenarios are too numerous to mention and are dealt with on a case-by-case basis when the lender is underwriting a borrower's creditworthiness. Not all lenders recognize or allow co-tenancy as an acceptable form of ownership. It is up to the lender to decide which structure provides the best guaranty of the loan. For example, Fannie Mae offers a multifamily program that allows tenancy in common or TICs as a form of ownership only if the co-tenants meet the following requirements:

> Co-tenants may be an eligible Borrower if: a) no more than five (5) co-tenants comprise the Borrower; b) no co-tenant is an individual; and c) each co-tenant is a single asset entity. If a tenancy-in-common agreement exists, the Lender must verify

that such agreement provides that: a) the Key Principal(s) has sufficient control to satisfy any Internal Revenue Service requirements; b) the Key Principal(s) has buy-out rights as to any other co-tenant and is financially able to effect such a buy-out; c) the Key Principal(s) has been named as the party to receive all notices or other communication from the Lender on behalf of all co-tenants; d) and each co-tenant has waived any Lien or partition rights or remedies against all other co-tenants. (Section 402.02, Co-Tenant Borrowers 10/01/07)

Partnerships

The most common form of ownership is a *partnership*. A partnership is an association of two or more persons to carry on a business for profit as owners. Though unincorporated, a partnership is a distinct entity consisting of partners that are natural persons or legal entities or a combination of both. For example, a partner may be any one of the following: an individual, corporation, trust, estate, executor, administrator, nominee, limited partnership, limited liability company, governmental agency, or any other legal or commercial entity. A partnership is generally classified as either a general partnership or a limited partnership, though there are a few other types, such as joint ventures, that are not as widely used in commercial real estate transactions. Though partnerships are most often formed for non–real estate business ventures, borrowers find them just as useful and beneficial for the purchase and ownership of commercial properties. When a partnership is formed for the sole purpose of owning and operating a single commercial property, the partnership is sometimes referred to as a single-asset entity (SAE) or special-purpose entity (SPE). Technically, a single-asset entity is not the same as a special-purpose entity, but what they do have in common, in the context of commercial real estate loans, is that they both typically are composed of a single asset such as a retail center, office building, or apartment complex. The technical or legal aspect that distinguishes a single-asset entity from a special-purpose entity is a topic of conversation best left to the legal profession. Within these two general categories of partnerships, there are some variant forms of partnerships that provide different tax and liability protections; however, the differences are technical and not germane to the purpose and scope of this chapter.

General Partnerships

A *general partnership* is the simplest form of partnership in terms of organizational structure and tax reporting. A general partnership is created when two or more persons form a business for profit. Neither a written partnership agreement nor a state-filing with the state's office of secretary of state is required to form a general partnership. However, if the partnership is conducted under an assumed name (a name that does not include the surname of all of the partners), then an assumed name certificate should be filed. Without state filing requirements in any local, county, or state government office, it is often difficult to ascertain if a general partnership even exists. Most likely, a general partnership is operating under a DBA (doing-business-as), a fictitious or assumed name that gives the partnership an identity. That name may or may not make it obvious that the entity is a general partnership. For example, a business name like Allied Associates or Brown & Company does not include any wording that indicates whether it is a general partnership. It may very well be just a sole proprietorship. Some names, however, do make it obvious that the business is in fact a general partnership. Names like "Evergreen Partners" or "Allied Associates, a Texas partnership," indicate that there is intent by at least two individuals to share in the profits of the business.

General partnerships conducting business under an assumed name, a DBA, or a fictitious name (as used by some states) must file an assumed name or fictitious name certificate in the office of the county clerk in each county where the partners maintain business premises. Filing an assumed name certificate does not necessarily establish the legality of a partnership unless the requisite elements of a partnership exist. Unlike tenancy in common, title to commercial property acquired with general partnership assets is held in the name of the general partnership. In other words, title is vested in the name given to the general partnership and not in the personal names of any of the individual partners. In this situation, the only name that appears in the title or deed is the general partnership name. As in tenancy-in-common ownership, title is held in each co-tenant's name individually, meaning that both names will appear on the title or deed. This distinction is important because the same two people can own property as tenants in common or as a general partnership.

Though not required by state law, a general partnership should have a written partnership agreement that governs the relationship between the individual partners and the partnership (a lender will not lend money to a general partnership in absence of a written partnership agreement). Without a partnership agreement, all partners by default have equal rights in the management and conduct of the business, with all decisions made by the consent of the majority of the partners. Also, without a partnership agreement, each partner shares equally in the profits without regard to different capital contributions made by each partner. For example, if one partner contributes more than half of the money or capital to the partnership, that partner will still receive only a prorated share of the profits based on number of partners, not on his share of the capital that was contributed. In this situation, if there are only four partners, the partner who contributed all of the money will get only 25 percent of the profits because of the absence of a written partnership agreement that divides ownership interests and capital contributions. If such a partnership agreement existed, the partner who put up all of the capital would have gotten all of the profits. Unless there are some mitigating circumstances, nearly all lenders require general partnerships to have partnership agreements.

A general partnership offers the least amount of liability protection for its individual partners and is usually not recommended for the purchase and ownership of commercial properties. The partnership is generally liable for loss or injury as a result of the actions of its partners if the actions were in the ordinary course of business of the partnership. Claims against the partnership may be enforced by suing the partnership and any or all of the partners, thus making the partners personally liable, jointly and severally, for all debts and obligations of the partnership.

Limited Partnerships

A *limited partnership* is a partnership formed by two or more persons with at least one person serving as the general partner (referred to as the GP) and at least one person participating as a limited partner, or a passive participant. As with a general partnership, a partner in a limited partnership may be an individual, trust, estate, corporation, limited partnership, limited liability company, custodian, trustee, executor, administrator, foreign limited partnership, or any commercial entity. The operative word in the term "limited partnership" is "limited." Unlike a general partnership, a limited partnership must designate a general partner, called the GP, who controls the partnership, while all other partners remain passive, meaning that they do not participate in the management and decision-making activities of the business. The general partner is the controlling or managing partner who actively participates in the control of the business, such as buying, selling, and mortgaging property and handling the money.

The limited partner is a passive investor who is silent and prefers only to contribute capital to the partnership and nothing more.

Limited partnerships are generally created with the intent to afford its participants the benefits of limited liability without the double taxation that occurs when taxes are imposed at the corporate level and then again at the shareholder level. In most cases, a limited partner has limited liability and is not liable for the debts and obligations of the partnership unless the limited partner happens to also be the general partner. In other words, a limited partner is insulated or shielded from all debts and obligations incurred by the partnership. The general partner, on the other hand, is totally responsible and liable for all acts, omissions, errors, and debts of the partnership. The general partner is usually the key principal within the partnership and is responsible for finding and putting together all of the individual investors who essentially participate as limited partners. In exchange for the personal liability that goes along with being the general partner, the general partner is granted generally unfettered authority over all decisions regarding day-to-day operations and capital expenditures on behalf of the partnership. Unlike a partner within a general partnership, a general partner (GP) within a limited partnership does not need approval from the majority of the partners in order to carry out most of his duties. The other advantage of a limited partnership is that all of the net income or profit from operations is passed through to the individual partners. Generally speaking, partners in a limited partnership are taxed the same way as partners in a general partnership. This is in contrast to a C-corporation. Income of a C-corporation is taxed both to the corporation and then to the shareholders, resulting in double taxation. This double taxation does not occur in either a limited partnership or a general partnership.

The formation of a domestic limited partnership requires a partnership agreement between the general partner and the limited partners. In order for a limited partnership to be legally recognized by the Internal Revenue Service, a certificate of formation must be filed with the office of the Secretary of State in the state where the entity is formed. The typical organizational structure of a limited partnership includes a single general partner with at least a 1 percent ownership interest and two to three limited partners with a combined ownership interest of 99 percent. The total ownership interest between the general partner and the limited partners must equal 100 percent. There can be many variations in individual ownership percentages. A general partner will generally have an ownership interest of 1 percent or higher, but it can be as little as 0.1 percent. Limited partners can each own as little as one-tenth of one percent (0.1%) or as much as 99 percent of the partnership. No matter how many limited partners there are, their total or aggregate ownership interests can never exceed 99 percent because the general partner is required by law to own at least 1 percent of the partnership (though there are exceptions where that percentage can be lower). Figure 6-1 illustrates the organizational structure of a limited partnership composed of both individuals and legal entities. The organizational structure illustrated in Figure 6-1 is just one of many possibilities.

With regard to real estate loans, a lender can look only to the general partner for a full and unconditional guarantee and repayment of the real estate loan. Even though the general partner typically has only a minority ownership interest, she always remains fully liable for the loan. General partners usually have very little equity or ownership interest in the partnership, which is why they are extremely reluctant to personally shoulder the burden of guaranteeing the entire loan. It is for this reason that general partners insist that the limited partnership (being the borrowing entity) borrow money only on a nonrecourse basis. A nonrecourse loan releases a general partner from liability and effectively prevents the lender from pursuing the general partner personally for the repayment of the loan or loss-

Figure 6-1. Organizational Structure of a Limited Partnership.

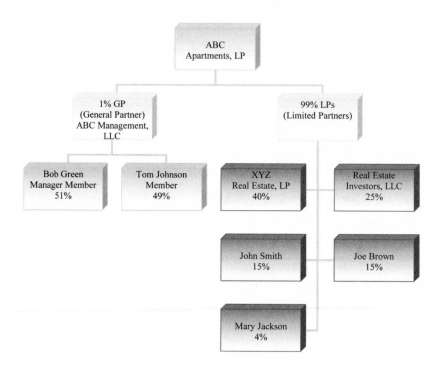

es in the event of default or foreclosure of the property. The only legal recourse a lender has with a nonrecourse loan is foreclosure of the property. Essentially, the general partner is protected from the lender if the limited partnership defaults on the loan. However, if the limited partnership cannot find a nonrecourse real estate loan, then the general partner will have no other choice but to personally guarantee the loan. If the general partner is willing to guarantee the loan, she will need to have a net worth at least equal to or greater than the loan amount; otherwise, the lender may require an additional guarantor. Most often, general partners are not willing or are not financially strong enough to singlehandedly guarantee the loan. When that situation occurs, a limited partner may need to be added as an additional guarantor, though this rarely happens, because limited partners are extremely adverse to any degree of liability, no matter how small.

Limited Liability Companies

Limited liability companies (LLCs) combine the most attractive feature of corporations, which is limited liability, and the most attractive feature of limited partnerships, which is pass-through of income and tax liability. An LLC resembles a corporation principally in its management structure and liability characteristics. Like a limited partnership, a limited liability company shields its owners from personal liability and passes all tax liabilities and benefits through to the owners. It is important to note that not all states recognize limited liability companies. Members of an LLC conducting business in those states may become liable for actions of the limited liability company, which is why, in the absence of personal limited liability, it is better in such situations to form a limited partnership.

Limited liability companies are typically composed of two or more owners and are commonly referred to as multimember LLCs. When a limited liability company is composed of only one owner, it is more appropriately referred to as a single-member LLC. A single-member LLC can also be owned by a husband and wife. A single-member LLC is often formed when a husband and wife want to own real estate together as community property without the exposure of personal liability. When it comes to federal income tax treatment, a single-member LLC by default is considered a sole proprietorship unless the sole member or married couple elects to treat the single-member LLC as a partnership. If the single-member LLC is treated as a partnership, the owner must file a partnership tax return (IRS Form 1065); otherwise, the income is simply reported on the owner's personal tax return (IRS Form 1040, Schedule C). A multiple-member LLC by default is treated as a partnership and must report income on a partnership tax return (IRS Form 1065) unless the owners elect to treat the multimember LLC as a C-corporation LLC.

A limited liability company is an attractive form of ownership for passive investments, venture capital projects, oil and gas projects, and, of course, commercial real estate ventures in which all of the owners desire limited liability. An LLC is owned by its members in either a passive or an active role. Members are effectively shareholders whose liability to other members is limited to the amounts of their agreed-upon capital contribution. Generally speaking, members are not liable at all to third parties for the debts and other obligations of the LLC. LLCs typically have one or more managers or managing members. It is also important to point out that the manager does not have to be a member of the LLC; in other words, the manager does not have to have an ownership interest in the LLC and can be merely a person entrusted with managing the company. The role of a managing member is similar to the role of a general partner of a limited partnership. Both are given authority to conduct the business affairs of the partnership on behalf of the partners, members, and the company as a whole.

The operation and management of the limited liability company are similar to those of a corporation. Instead of articles of incorporation, a limited liability company files articles of organization or a certificate of formation that provides the name of the limited liability company, the anticipated duration of the company, the name and address of the registered agent, and the names of the managers. Also, instead of bylaws, the limited liability company has what is known as "regulations," a "company agreement," or an "operating agreement," which governs the management and operation of the company. Owners of the limited liability company are referred to as members instead of shareholders. Also, instead of having directors as with a corporation, limited liability companies elect managers at their annual meetings. Managers effectively manage the business of the LLC and are authorized to designate or appoint company officers.

In spite of the limited liability afforded to all members, commercial real estate lenders nevertheless require a personal guarantee from all managing members for the full and unconditional repayment of the loan, unless of course the loan is nonrecourse. Lenders typically need only one person to guarantee the loan, assuming that there is only one managing member. However, if there are two or more managing members, all will need to personally guarantee the loan because of their controlling interest in the company. Occasionally, lenders will require an additional guarantor if the sole guarantee of the managing member(s) is considered inadequate. If this situation occurs, the lender may require some of the members to step up and guarantee the loan, as well. No matter who the guarantors are, lenders will always underwrite any member that has greater than a 20 percent ownership interest in the limited liability company.

Corporations

Another form of ownership that can own commercial property and borrow money is a *corporation*. Corporations are artificial entities created by state law. They are designed to be legally separate and apart from their owners or shareholders. A corporation can acquire and sell commercial real estate, enter into contracts, and sue and be sued in its own name theoretically without risk or liability conferred upon the shareholders. Shareholders in a corporation elect a board of directors at least once a year; this board then appoints officers to manage and operate the corporation. The officers are responsible for the day-to-day management of the corporation, and the board of directors is responsible for overseeing the officers on a broader scope.

In order to legally form a corporation, the owners or shareholders must prepare a set of documents called articles of incorporation or a certificate of formation and file it with the office of the Secretary of State in the state where the entity is formed. They must also draft a set of bylaws and elect the board of directors. The board of directors, as noted, then appoints officers of the corporation, such as the president, treasurer, CEO, and CFO. There are several types of corporations, such as a C-corporation, close corporations, Subchapter S corporation, and one-person corporations. The type of corporation most commonly used by real estate investors is the one-person corporation, where the sole shareholder also serves as the sole director and officer of the corporation. With this type of one-person corporation, the sole shareholder is in theory operating as a sole proprietorship with the benefits of a corporate entity, thereby limiting the liability of the owner. A majority of corporations are more complex than the one-person corporation and are not necessarily formed just for the sole purpose of investing in commercial real estate. All corporations, whether they are owned by one shareholder or hundreds of shareholders, offer limited liability with regard to corporate debts. The shareholders, officers, and directors are not liable for the debts of the corporation so long as the shareholders treat the corporation as a separate entity; therefore, creditors can pursue only the corporation for the corporation's debts. In some circumstances, a creditor may be able to pierce the corporate veil that shields the shareholders from the corporation's debts; if that happens, shareholders are jointly and severally liable for all of the debts of the corporation. This is why LLCs are almost uniformly preferred over corporations unless there is some overriding tax reason to form a corporation, since there can be no real "piercing" of LLCs.

The most notable monetary disadvantage of a corporation is that it is subject to double taxation. A corporation is taxed on its net income; then shareholders are taxed again on the dividends paid or distributed to them by the corporation. However, if the corporation elects to be classified as a Subchapter S corporation, the tax at the corporate level can be eliminated, leaving taxes to be paid only at the shareholder level. Under the IRS rules, a Subchapter S election allows a corporation to be treated as a partnership for tax purposes while at the same time retaining the advantage of limited liability for its shareholders. When a corporation converts to a Subchapter S corporation, it essentially becomes a conduit of income or losses directly to the shareholders, just like a partnership.

Corporations that want to borrow money for the purchase of commercial real estate are essentially treated by lenders the same as general partnerships, limited partnerships, and limited liability companies. Unless the corporation has more than one asset, significant stockholder's equity, and plenty of liquidity (cash), a lender will usually require a personal guarantee of the loan. As with all of the other types of ownership entities, the lender will underwrite all of the shareholders who have more than a 20 percent ownership interest in the corporation. Whether or not all of the shareholders will need to personally guarantee the loan is a decision only the lender can make. The number of guarantors needed to guarantee the loan is a function of the financial strength of the guarantors as a whole. In general, when a commercial real estate loan is a full-recourse loan, the lender will require a "warm body," which is industry jargon for an individual or person who can personally pay back the loan with his own assets in the event the lender tries to foreclose on the property. It is rare that any of the corporate officers or even the shareholders will agree to personally guarantee a commercial real estate loan or, for that matter, any business loan on behalf of the corporation. Most often, if a corporation cannot provide the lender with a corporate guarantee that might otherwise eliminate the need for a personal guarantee, it is highly unlikely the lender will approve the loan. A corporate guarantee is just as good as a personal guarantee if the company has sufficient assets and liquidity to pay back the loan; however, that is not usually the case with a one-person corporation. Usually, the only way for a corporation to obtain loan approval in the absence of either a corporate guarantee or a personal guarantee of the loan is to take the loan on a nonrecourse basis, meaning the lender can look only as far as the property itself as sole collateral for the repayment of the loan in the event of default and foreclosure.

Trusts

The final and most commonly misunderstood type of ownership is a trust. A trust is a legal entity created to hold assets for the benefit of certain persons or entities. In the simplest terms, a trust is an arrangement whereby real property (tangible and intangible) is managed by one person (or persons or organizations) for the benefit of another. A trust is created by a settlor, who entrusts some or all of his or her property to people of his choice, referred to as the trustee. In the United States, the settlor is also called the trustor, grantor, donor, or creator. A trust may have one or multiple trustees, and the trustee can be either a person or a legal entity such as a company. The trustee's role is to manage the trust and to hold legal title to the trust property for the benefit of one or more individuals or organizations, referred to as the beneficiary, usually specified by the settlor. The trust is governed by the terms of the trust document or trust agreement, which is usually written and occasionally set out in deed form.

There are approximately a dozen or so different types of trusts, though only two are worth mentioning with regard to commercial real estate loans. When the word "trust" is used, it is often associated with the words "revocable" or "irrevocable." Revocable and irrevocable trusts are the most common type of trusts encountered by commercial real estate lenders. A revocable trust can be changed, amended, altered, or revoked by its settlor at any time, provided the settlor is not mentally incapacitated. In lieu of a last will and testament, revocable trusts are becoming increasingly common in the United States because they minimize the administrative costs associated with probate and provide centralized administration of a person's final affairs after death. An irrevocable trust is generally more complex than a revocable trust and under normal circumstances cannot be changed by the trustee or the beneficiaries of the trust. In other words, the terms of an irrevocable trust cannot be amended or revised until the terms or purposes of the trust have been completed. Although, in rare cases, a court may change the terms of the trust due to unexpected changes in circumstances that make the trust uneconomical or unwieldy to administer.

Trusts can borrow money for the purchase of commercial real estate the same way that partnerships, limited liability companies, and corporations can, as long as there is an individual or warm body to personally guarantee the loan. The warm body or guarantor within a trust is always the trustee and sometimes the settlor or trustor, as well. Trustees are treated no differently from individuals, general partners, or managing members and must endure the same financial scrutiny by lenders and their underwriters. Lending to a trust requires the same level of due diligence as with any other legal entity. In regard to underwriting, lenders often require a complete set of trust documents. A complete set of trust documents will include the following:

- ➢ Name of the trust
- ➢ Names of the trustees
- ➢ Powers of the trustees
- ➢ Signature page of the trustees with notarizations
- ➢ Copy of trust agreement and all amendments
- ➢ Trust borrowing authorization (signed and notarized)
- ➢ Certification of trust (signed and notarized)

> ➤ Trust guarantee certification (required if trust is guarantor)

The trust itself will also be required to submit financial statements (P&Ls) at the entity level as well as tax returns for the previous two years.

The average lender is able to loan money to a trust, regardless of the number of individual assets owned by the trust primarily because of the personal guarantee. However, there are some lenders that will not loan money to certain trusts. For example, agency lenders, such as Fannie Mae and Freddie Mac, that offer non-recourse apartment loans prefer only to lend to single-asset entities (SAE). A single-asset entity subject to this narrow lending restriction required by agency lenders such as Freddie Mac and Fannie Mae is what real estate attorneys refer to as a bankruptcy remote entity. Bankruptcy remote means that a single and only asset held in the trust is insulated from the trustees' other creditors. A trust can own one or even multiple properties. A trust or any legal entity, for that matter, that owns a single property is referred to as single-asset entity or special-purpose entity. However, most trusts own more than one asset, and thus rarely ever qualify as single-asset entities.

INDEX

Look for These Informative AMACOM Titles at www.amacombooks.org:

Decoding the New Mortgage Market by David Reed $17.95

Financing Your Condo, Coop, or Townhouse by David Reed $18.95

An Insider's Guide to Refinancing Your Mortgage by David Reed $16.95

The Landlord's Financial Tool Kit by Michael C. Thomsett $18.95

Mortgages 101, Second Edition by David Reed $16.95

Mortgage Confidential by David Reed $16.95

Navigating the Mortgage Minefield by Richard Giannamore and Barbara Bardow Osach $17.95

The Property Management Tool Kit by Mike Beirne $19.95

The Real Estate Investor's Pocket Calculator by Michael C. Thomsett $17.95

Saving the Deal by Tracey Rumsey $17.95

Stop Foreclosure Now by Lloyd Segal $19.95

The Successful Landlord by Ken Roth $19.95

Your Successful Career as a Mortgage Broker by David Reed $18.95

Your Eco-Friendly Home by Sid Davis $17.95